It's Easy to Make Conversation

Proven Conversation Starters, Listening Skills, and Recovery Strategies to Talk with Confidence in Networking, Friendship, and Work

George Munson

GL DIGITAL PUBLISHING LLC

Contents

Introduction

You're at the edge of a crowded room, your nametag crooked and your hands sweaty as you hold your phone. It looks like everyone else moves easily from group to group, laughing, making plans, and sharing stories. Meanwhile, your mind is full of worries: What if people think you're awkward? What if you say the wrong thing? Or what if you don't say anything at all? You take a breath, look for a chance to join in, but freeze. The moment passes, and you tell yourself you'll try again next time. This book is here to help you with that struggle to connect.

If this sounds familiar, you're not alone. I know that sinking feeling. I used to dread parties, trip over my words in meetings, and leave group chats unread. For a long time, I thought some people were just naturally charming, and the rest of us struggled. But after I lost a job because I "didn't connect well in the interview," I knew I had to change for the sake of my career, my peace of mind, and my happiness. I started learning what makes conversations work and why so many people find them hard. The main thing I learned is that anyone can improve their social confidence with practice and the right help, step by step, small changes add up to big results.

Conversation skills aren't just a bonus; they're key to success and happiness. Research shows that strong social skills help people get hired faster, earn more promotions, and feel more satisfied. One Harvard study found that 85% of job success comes from people skills. Still, many people feel anxious or unsure about starting conversations or joining groups. This book is here to help you build comfort, connection, and confidence.

If you've tried to fix this by reading a social skills book, you might have ended up discouraged. Maybe you've heard advice like "just be yourself," "smile more," or "ask open-ended questions." These tips mean well, but they don't always help when you're facing a room full of strangers or trying to recover from an awkward silence. Most books skip the real-life details, like how to join a fast-moving group at work, what to do when someone gives you a one-word answer, or how to make friends in a new city. Digital communication is another challenge. Where are the scripts for Slack, Instagram, or group texts full of inside jokes? If you've checked the reviews, you'll see that many people feel the same way.

That's why I wrote this book: to give you real, practical tools for how we communicate today, both in person and online. These tools are designed to help you see tangible progress, making social confidence feel more attainable and less overwhelming.

If you're skeptical, I get it. Maybe advice felt fake or forced, and you worry you'll never be "good at people." The truth: social confidence is a skill anyone can build. Small steps, practiced often, create big changes. This book will guide you through micro-challenges and new scripts for real results. My promise is practical transformation, not just theory.

Here's what you'll find in this book. First, we'll look at conversation starters and icebreakers that feel real, not awkward. Then we'll dive into active listening and nonverbal cues, because what you don't say is just as important as what you do. We'll talk about handling awkward or tough conversations, bouncing back from social setbacks, and keeping things going even when you feel stuck. There are chapters on joining group chats, both online and in person, on cultural differences, and on making a strong impression at work or in interviews. You'll also get a toolkit for digital communication, including DM etiquette, video call tips, and ways to stay connected in a fast-paced world.

By the end of this book, you'll have conversation starters you can use right away, challenges to build your confidence, digital strategies, and your own personalized "social playbook." You can use these tools whether you're going to a networking event, texting a new friend, or just hoping to feel less awkward at a family dinner.

Here's what I ask: really try these strategies. Try something new from each chapter. Notice every change, even the small ones. Each conversation is a step toward real confidence and connection. You don't have to be perfect. Just show up and see how you grow.

Chapter One

The Modern Conversation Landscape

A friend once told me he spent twenty minutes at a work event pretending to scroll through his phone, trying to figure out how to join a group but never finding the courage to do so. He left feeling invisible. Many of us know this feeling, leaving a party, group chat, or comment thread, unsure how to fit in. These moments are happening more often as the unwritten rules for conversation keep changing. Connecting at work, with friends, and online is now more complicated than ever. We have to read moods quickly, pick up on cues over text and video, and adjust to different cultures. One moment you're joking in a group chat full of memes, and the next, you're serious in a Zoom call with your boss's boss. This chapter examines how socializing has changed and why old advice often no longer works.

Why "Just Be Yourself" Isn't Enough Anymore

You've probably heard the advice, "Just be yourself!" as the answer to social problems. At first, it sounds comforting. But if you walk into a room full of strangers, you'll often see it lead to awkward silence. That advice made sense when social circles were small, and most people shared the same norms. Back then, being yourself worked because everyone understood the same unwritten rules.

Today, our social lives include school friends, coworkers, online contacts, and people from different cultures or generations. What works in one group can easily go wrong in another. For example, some group chats are full of quick jokes and inside references, while others are more reserved. If you bring your unfiltered self, maybe you're blunt or sarcastic, it can confuse or push away people who don't share your background. It's not just about personality; culture matters too. How you act in a New York or Mumbai office might not work in Tokyo or Berlin. Even the meaning of emojis can change depending on who you're talking to.

Social roles are more flexible now. We switch between being a networker, friend, coworker, group member, or mentor, and each role has its own way of interacting. At work, you might be professional and focused, but with friends, you're more relaxed and playful. Changing how you act isn't being fake; it's just adjusting to the situation. You probably don't joke with your boss the same way you do with your best friend. Digital communication makes things trickier because texts and messages can be misunderstood, and mistakes can stick around.

To handle these changing roles well, you need to be both genuine and flexible. The advice to "just be yourself" ignores the fact that your identity shifts depending on the situation, a skill called code-switching. It's like adjusting a radio to get the right station for each setting. This means knowing when to be formal, when to listen, or when to keep things short, all while staying true to your values.

Simple advice often misses the real challenge: reading the room. Sometimes you need to match the group's mood, joining in when everyone is energetic or staying calm when things are serious. Reading the room means noticing when people are done with small talk or when silence shows they're thinking, not uncomfortable. Understanding these details is important, especially since silence or body language can mean different things in different cultures. With these skills, conversations get easier and feel more natural.

So what really helps? Having practical strategies for different situations, such as starting conversations at work or reaching out online. That's what you'll find here: tools for reading the mood, finding ways to join in, and changing your approach when things aren't going well. Remember, social skills are learnable, and practicing these strategies will help you improve over time.

Try This "Context Tuning" Exercise

Here's an exercise to help you become more adaptable:

For the next three days, choose one daily interaction at work (or school), one with friends (even online), and one with someone new (like a cashier). Before each, pause for five seconds and ask yourself, "What does this situation need? Should I be formal or casual? Should I speak up or listen first?" Pay attention to how you adjust your approach and how people react. Write down what felt comfortable or awkward, such as whether you felt confident initiating or listening. You're not changing who you are, just figuring out which parts of yourself fit best in each situation.

Instead of relying on old advice that doesn't really help, you'll build real skills for connecting genuinely and effectively. Remember, every small step you take can boost your confidence and show that change is possible.

Debunking the "Born Conversationalist" Myth

You've probably met someone who seems to move through every conversation with ease, like it's natural for them. Maybe you've thought, "I'll never be like that. I'm just not built for it." This idea is common: that some people are born social butterflies, while others always feel left out. But here's the truth: nobody is born knowing how to work a crowd or light up a group chat. The people who seem natural have actually spent time practicing, making mistakes, and learning from awkward moments. Even some of the best communicators started shy. Warren Buffett, for example, was once so afraid of public speaking that he would sweat just thinking about it. Oprah Winfrey, now a famous talk show host, grew up feeling out of place and unheard. They didn't suddenly become great at socializing; they practiced, learned from their mistakes, and kept trying. Social skills are learnable, and consistent effort can help you improve just like them.

Science weighs in on this, too. The concept of neuroplasticity, the brain's ability to form and reorganize connections throughout life, proves that you're never stuck with your current skill set (How clinicians can support neuroplasticity in adults, n.d.). Learning new conversation skills isn't just for kids or outgoing types. Adults can literally rewire their brains through practice and feedback. Whether you're an introvert who loves quiet or someone who's always been told you talk too much, your social "muscle" can grow stronger with use. Brain scans show that social interaction triggers chemical changes that, over time, improve memory and emotional intelligence.

So what really makes someone good at conversation? It's not a special gene or some secret charm. The real keys are practice, feedback, and taking time to think about what works and what doesn't. It's like learning to play the guitar; most people can't play a song perfectly on their first try. They make mistakes, repeat the same chords, and listen to others' advice. Conversation works the same way. The more you put yourself in situations where you need to connect, like chatting with a barista or messaging a coworker, the more comfortable you'll get. Feedback is important too; friends, mentors, or even strangers can show you what works and what doesn't. Thinking about awkward moments with curiosity, not shame, helps you improve: Why did that joke fall flat? What made the group go quiet? When you look at these moments as learning opportunities, you get better.

Your environment shapes your social confidence much more than any so-called natural talent. Maybe you grew up in a loud, lively home where jumping into conversations was normal. Or maybe your family was quiet or didn't encourage you to speak up. These early experiences affect how you see yourself socially, but they don't decide your future. You can build new habits no matter where you began.

Many people get stuck in negative thinking: "I'm just not a people person." "I always say the wrong thing." "Nobody wants to listen to me." These thoughts feel true because repeating them makes them part of your self-image. But what if you replaced them with more helpful beliefs? Try these instead: "I can learn to connect with practice." "Everyone says the wrong thing sometimes; it's normal." "Most people are too busy thinking about themselves to judge me." When you notice yourself thinking in extremes, pause and ask: Is this really true, or just a habit?

You might still wonder whether someone shy, awkward, or quiet can really improve. The answer is yes, and I've seen it happen many times. For example, I once coached a college student who always kept to herself. She started by saying hello to classmates, then joined study groups. After a few months, she felt confident enough to organize weekend meetups. Or think about an engineer who dreaded team meetings so much that he pretended to have technical problems to avoid video calls. With gentle feedback and practice in low-pressure settings, like group chats about hobbies, he slowly found his voice and became the person everyone turned to for onboarding new hires. Next, we'll look at how progress happens over time.

Progress doesn't happen overnight; it's more like a slow climb than a quick race. Some days will be frustrating, and you'll replay awkward moments, wishing you could do them over. Other days, you'll surprise yourself by making someone laugh or joining a conversation without overthinking. Every small step counts. Even one new connection or a good group chat can boost your confidence for weeks.

If you still feel unsure, maybe you've tried before and felt stuck, remember that every skill takes steady, honest effort. The main point is that conversation isn't something you're just born with; it's learned by trying things out, accepting feedback, and practicing. Growth is possible for anyone willing to keep trying, even if it feels hard right now.

Busting the "I'm Just Not Social" Myth

It's easy to believe that social skills are for other people, the ones who breeze through parties, always have something to say, and make friends without trying. You might think, "That's just not me. I'm not social. I wasn't made for this." But that's just a myth, and it stops many people from making the connections they want. The truth is, being good in social situations isn't a fixed trait like eye color or height. It's a skill, and like any skill, you can learn it. Your brain isn't stuck; it changes with every new experience. This is called neuroplasticity, which means your mind can form new pathways as you practice new behaviors and ways of thinking, regardless of age. It's like leveling up in a game: the more you practice, the stronger your "social muscle" gets.

I knew someone who used to hide by the snack table at every party and only spoke when someone first talked to him. Over time, he tried small things, like complimenting someone's shoes or asking about the music. These little steps helped him build confidence. It didn't happen overnight, but eventually he became known for hosting great game nights where everyone felt welcome. What changed wasn't his personality, but his willingness to replace the old story of "I'm not social" with "I can get better at this." Each new try helped his brain get used to social situations and feel less nervous about the unknown.

Many people think being introverted means you can't connect with others, but that's not true. Being introverted means you recharge best alone or in quiet settings; it doesn't say anything about your social skills. In fact, many introverts are great at one-on-one conversations or at connecting deeply with a small group. If you've ever felt tired after a big event but energized by a good talk with a close friend, you're not alone. Sometimes the loudest person in the room is the least connected, while the quiet observer is building strong relationships in their own way.

Try this:

Imagine a flowchart with three branches: Introvert, Extrovert, and Social Chameleon. If you like alone time but enjoy meaningful conversations, you're on the introvert branch. If you love crowds and constant talking, you're probably more extroverted. If you switch between both depending on your mood or the situation, you're a social chameleon. There's no wrong answer. The real key is knowing your style and using your strengths. I know an introvert who never liked big gatherings but became famous for her coffee meetups and thoughtful texts. Her friends trust her with secrets because she listens closely and remembers what matters. She shows that "not social" is just a label that doesn't match real life.

People connect in many different ways. Some are storytellers, while others are good listeners. Some love the energy of groups, while others prefer talking in pairs or small groups. Some even famous people don't fit the "life of the party" image. Emma Watson has said she feels shy in crowds but shines in meaningful conversations about causes she cares about. Keanu Reeves is known for being quiet and private, but he connects genuinely with people on set and with fans. These examples show there isn't just one way to be "social." You probably have your own style, even if you haven't used it much yet.

You might still worry that this book won't help you, even though other advice hasn't worked before. Maybe you tried a networking tip or two, and nothing changed, or you felt even more out of place after trying to act like someone else. Here's what's different: research shows that small, steady practice makes a bigger difference than any personality test or self-help slogan. Studies on building skills show that repetition, not natural talent, leads to improvement over time (How clinicians can support neuroplasticity in adults, n.d.). Even if it feels awkward at first, showing up again and again builds new habits and helps your brain get used to social situations.

So here's my suggestion: Treat this book as an experiment, not a test you have to pass right away. Try the 7-day Social Experiment described here. For one week, do one small thing each day that pushes you a little outside your comfort zone, like giving a quick compliment to a barista, replying in a group chat instead of just watching, or sending a friendly message to someone you admire online. Keep track of how it feels and what happens. You'll probably find that some things go better than you expected, while others might not work out, but none of it defines you in the long run. Social confidence grows with each new try, and every step helps you build real connections, even if you've always thought "I'm just not social."

The Fear of Rejection, or Why It's Normal and How to Shrink It

You're standing outside a conference room, badge around your neck, repeating your introduction in your head for the tenth time. You want to say hello, but you can't seem to move. Your heart pounds and your palms sweat, almost like you're standing on a cliff. Why does something as simple as greeting someone feel so scary? The fear of being ignored or rejected can stop even the most prepared person. This isn't a mistake; it's your brain's old survival system at work. Long ago, being rejected by your group could mean losing safety or support. Our brains still see social rejection as a threat, making us notice every possible snub, even at a networking event or in a group chat. That's why one awkward silence or a non-response can stick with you all day, even if it meant nothing to the other person.

This old survival instinct still shows up today. At a networking event, you might see a lively group and feel like there's an invisible wall stopping you from joining. Your mind jumps to the worst-case scenarios: What if they turn away? What if I mess up my words? You might even remember past rejections, which makes you even more nervous. But here's what most people don't realize: everyone else is dealing with these feelings too. The real difference is in how we handle them, not whether we have them.

So how can you make the fear smaller? First, remember that rejection isn't a judgment about who you are; it's just information. Sometimes it means nothing; maybe the person was busy, distracted, or just having a bad day. Instead of seeing a "no" or an ignored message as proof you're not good enough, try changing your perspective. I like the saying "Rejection = Redirection." When something doesn't work out, it can lead you to better opportunities. For example, if you reach out to a colleague online and they never reply, it might hurt at first, but maybe that conversation wasn't meant to happen. Over time, you might find a group that fits you much better. I've seen people get ignored by one group, only to find another where they're valued for who they are.

This is where your mindset makes a big difference. Instead of letting rejection turn into shame or self-doubt, treat each "no" as neutral feedback. It's not about you as a person; it's about timing, chemistry, or the situation. In fact, getting rejections can be a badge of honor. Every time you put yourself out there and don't get a response, it shows you're making progress. Building this tolerance is like working out a muscle; the more you face those small disappointments, the less they bother you.

If you want to grow braver, try the "Micro-Rejection Challenge." This is about intentionally seeking out small rejections in safe situations until they start to lose their edge. Here are five challenges to get you started:

- Ask a stranger for the time or directions, even if you already know the answer.

- Request a menu change at your favorite café (e.g., asking for oat milk instead of regular milk).

- Compliment someone in public and notice their reaction.

- DM someone you admire on social media with a quick thank-you or question.

- Offer to help in a group chat and see if anyone responds.

Each time you try one of these, write down what actually happened. Did anything terrible happen? Probably not. Most of the time, people are polite or just neutral, and sometimes they're even pleasantly surprised that you reached out.

It also helps to separate your sense of self from what happens in any one conversation. Too often, people tie their self-worth to a single outcome: If someone ignores me, I must be boring. If I'm rejected, I must be unlikable. That's not true; it's just a story your mind tells when it's trying to protect you. To change this, try a simple reflection exercise: After any social setback, big or small, write down what happened and what story you're telling yourself about it. Then ask: Is this story fair? Is there another way to see it? One reader shared that she tracked every rejection for a month and found that most were either neutral (people were busy) or positive (she learned something new). By separating facts from stories, she started to see these moments as small bumps rather than big obstacles.

The fear of rejection will never go away completely, but it doesn't have to control you. Every time you take a risk, future conversations get a little easier and less scary. The truth is, real connection comes from these brave moments; each small "no" brings you closer to the right "yes." So next time you feel anxious before speaking up or sending a message, remember your brain is just trying to protect you from a danger that isn't really there anymore. You can move forward anyway, using new mindsets and real skills to bounce back stronger each time.

Chapter Two

Breaking the Ice In Real Life (IRL) and Online

The Ultimate Icebreaker and Playbook for Any Situation

Everyone has experienced those awkward moments in a coffee shop line or at a party, wanting to start a conversation but not knowing what to say. It can be tough to break the silence, especially if you worry about sounding awkward. Having a few go-to icebreakers for different situations can make connecting with others much easier.

At parties, where meeting new people can feel tricky, try starting with specific questions like, "What brought you here tonight?" or "How do you know the host?" These open-ended questions make it easy for others to talk. You can also ask about the food, like, "Have you tried any snacks yet?" Noticing something about what someone is wearing and asking, "That's a great [item], where did you find it?" can also help start a conversation. Picking up on unique details gives you a natural way in.

On public transport, most people like their privacy, so keep things light and related to the moment. You might ask, "Is this your usual route?" or "Does this train always run late?" These are easy to answer and don't put pressure on anyone to keep talking. If you notice someone reading an interesting book or wearing unique headphones, you can ask, "Would you recommend that book?" or "Listening to anything good?"

Coffee shops are great places for casual chats, whether you're in line or sharing a table. You could ask, "What's your go-to order?" or "Is it always this busy?" If you see someone working on something, try, "That looks interesting. Are you working on something fun?" Keep it light; most people don't want to be grilled before they've had their coffee.

Online, icebreakers are just as important in group chats and virtual communities. Instead of asking "How's everyone?" which can feel impersonal, try something like, "What's the best thing that happened to you this week?" Being genuine and attentive helps your audience feel valued and encourages authentic sharing. If the group has a specific topic, ask for recommendations, like, "Played any good games recently?" Context is important online, too. Mentioning a meme, trend, or something familiar can help get people talking.

Good icebreakers fit the situation, invite more than a yes or no answer, and don't put anyone on the spot. The right question matches the place or moment. Open-ended questions help people share more and feel heard. Low-pressure questions let the conversation flow without big expectations. For example, "Nice weather today, huh?" is simple but boring. "What would your perfect weather day look like?" is much more interesting and makes your audience feel involved.

Try not to use generic lines. Some people like bold questions, such as, "If you could teleport anywhere, where would you go?" If you're more reserved, use an observation plus a question, like, "I noticed your laptop sticker, do you code?" This shows you're paying attention and invites the other person to share without any pressure.

Experiment with different approaches to find what works for you. Not every attempt will work, and sometimes people are just busy. Don't see silence as a failure; context and timing are important. Trying new methods helps your audience feel more confident and less discouraged when things don't go perfectly.

Build Your Personalized Icebreaker Toolkit

Think of three places you'll visit this week, like work, the gym, a café, or even an online chat. For each place, choose one bold and one subtle icebreaker you'd feel comfortable using. Give them a try, then write down what happened, even if nothing special happened. Pay attention to what felt natural and what felt awkward. With practice, you'll build your own set of go-to openers.

A good icebreaker isn't about impressing anyone. It's about making it easy to connect without pressure. Treat each try as a small experiment to build your confidence and connect with others. It gets easier the more you do it.

Conversation Starters That Actually Work at Networking Events

Walking into a networking event can feel awkward, almost like stepping onto a movie set without a script. You'll see groups of people talking, and it might seem like everyone already knows each other. But most people are just as nervous as you and are open to real conversations. Instead of asking, "So, what do you do?" try something more specific, like, "What's the most interesting project you've worked on recently?" This helps people share something meaningful and keeps things real. Another easy way to start is, "How did you hear about this event?" It's relevant and can lead to more conversation. If there's a keynote or panel, mention it: "Did you catch the last keynote? I found the part about remote teams useful, did you?" Talking about the event itself gives everyone something easy to discuss.

Don't stress about sounding perfect; networking isn't about having flawless lines. People can tell when an opener is rehearsed and usually ignore it. Focus on being real. If you notice you're sounding stiff, pause and show interest in the person you're talking to. Maybe you spot an interesting pin or a book they're holding: "I noticed your pin, does it have a special meaning?" Or if you hear someone mention a topic you care about, join in honestly: "I overheard you mention marketing, are you in that field too?" Being curious and genuine always works better than small talk that feels fake.

Networking conversations usually follow a rhythm: starting the chat, getting involved, and then wrapping up.

Entry

When you approach new groups or individuals, be confident but keep it simple. If someone is alone or a group looks welcoming, ask, "Mind if I join you?" This shows respect and interest. If they don't seem open, move on.

Engagement

Ask questions that invite stories or opinions, not just yes or no answers. For example, "What drew you to your field?" or "What has surprised you about your industry lately?" These kinds of questions help real conversations happen and keep things moving naturally.

Exit

Ending a conversation can feel awkward, but there are easy ways to do it. You could say, "I want to let you mingle, but it was great to meet you!" or "I promised myself I'd meet three new people tonight, thanks for being my first!" This leaves things on a good note and makes it easy to reconnect later.

After the Event

Many people forget to follow up after networking. You don't need a long message; send a quick note like, "Great meeting you at [event]; would love to stay in touch!" Mention something specific from your conversation, such as, "I enjoyed hearing your thoughts on remote work; let's connect on LinkedIn." If you're sending an email, keep it short and personal: "Hi [Name], I really enjoyed our chat about [topic] at [event]. Would love to keep in touch, here's my LinkedIn/email." Keeping it simple and memorable helps you stand out.

If you're connecting on LinkedIn, avoid using a generic template. Personalize your invitation by mentioning something you talked about: "Hi [Name], I enjoyed talking at [event], especially about marketing podcasts. Hope we can share more ideas! This shows you were paying attention and helps your request stand out.

Networking is more than just swapping business cards; it's about making real connections. When you're curious and genuine, you stand out, and people remember you for how you made them feel. Taking the chance to start new conversations and being yourself is the best way to connect and not just blend in. The main point: focus on building real relationships, not just surface-level ones.

Opening Lines That Don't Feel Weird

Starting a new conversation can make you nervous, your heart might race, and you might overthink what to say. This is totally normal and happens to everyone, even confident people. Usually, the worry is worse than what actually happens. Once you take the first step, most people are glad someone started talking.

When you're out alone in social settings, the best openers are simple and not too forward. For example, "Hey, I'm trying to meet more people tonight, what's your story?" works because it's honest and straightforward.

You don't need to come up with something clever, just be open about wanting to connect. If you like using humor, try, "This is my official attempt at not being a wallflower tonight." This can set a fun, relaxed mood if it fits your style.

If you're an introvert, it's okay to be gentle. Saying something like, "Hi, I never know how to start these things, but I figured I'd say hi," admits the awkwardness and takes the pressure off both people. This kind of honesty is often appreciated and can lead to a real conversation.

Tone and Body Language

Your tone is more important than having the perfect words. If you seem nervous or afraid of being rejected, people can pick up on it and might back off. Try to relax your body language, smile, and keep a comfortable posture. Match your tone to where you are: be casual in relaxed settings, and a bit more formal in professional ones. For example, "I'm new here and just wanted to introduce myself. What brings you to this event?" Don't stress about using fancy words; how you make someone feel matters most.

Handling Lukewarm Reactions

Sometimes people respond neutrally. They might be distracted or just not interested at the moment. Usually, this isn't about you or your opener; it's just a matter of timing or not clicking. If someone doesn't seem interested, say, "No worries, have a great night!" This keeps things smooth and avoids awkwardness.

Minimizing Rejection

Rejection feels less painful if you stop seeing it as a sign of your value. Most of the time, it's just about timing or whether you click. You can't control how others react, only how you approach things. Each time you try, it gets a little easier. Treat every opener as a small experiment, not something huge.

Calling Out the Awkwardness

Talking about the awkwardness directly can really help. If you're nervous, admit it: "I always feel awkward starting conversations at these things. Do you ever get that?" This can break the ice and help the other person relax, too.

Romantic and Professional Contexts

Romantic situations can feel riskier, but being simple and respectful is most important. Try, "Hey, I noticed your [band shirt/book/drink], and had to ask, are you a fan?" It's direct and personal, and lets the other person join in or politely step away. If they're not interested, don't stick around, nod and say, "No worries, enjoy your night." People appreciate that mix of confidence and respect.

In professional settings, show interest in what others do: "I'm new here and would love to hear about what you do." If the conversation slows down, end on a good note: "Thanks for chatting, I'll let you get back to mingling."

The Role of Self, Compassion

The key to all of this is being kind to yourself. No one is great at socializing every time. Even the best networkers have awkward or failed conversations. The more you practice, the less the misses matter, and the easier it gets.

DM Like a Pro: Opening Digital Conversations Without the Awkwardness

Sending a Direct Message (DM) or that first text can make you nervous. You might stare at your phone, type "hey" or "what's up," then delete it because it feels too plain. To get a real response, make your message personal. Generic greetings usually get ignored. Instead, mention something specific, like a recent Instagram story: "Saw your story from the mountains, did you find any cool trails?" This makes your message stand out. On LinkedIn, which is more professional, start with a compliment or mention something you have in common: "I enjoyed your post about remote teamwork; it got me thinking about my own habits."

Personalizing your message means more than just using someone's name or a fact. It's about making the other person feel noticed. The more specific you are, the more genuine you seem. Instead of just saying, "Hey," try, "Loved your photo from [event], was it as fun as it looked?" If you're networking, you could say, "Noticed we both follow [industry leader], have you found their advice helpful?" These kinds of openers show you want a real conversation, not just small talk.

Adjust your message for both the platform and the person. On Instagram, keep things casual and short, friendly and light works best. Long DMs are easy to skip. Match their style: if they use emojis or memes, add a few, but don't overdo it, especially at first. On LinkedIn, be a bit more structured and polished. Start with a greeting, explain why you're reaching out, and try not to sound too stiff: "Hi [Name], I saw you work in UX design at [Company]. I'm interested in that field. How did you get started?" Always match your tone to who you're talking to, whether it's a peer, mentor, or potential friend.

The length of your message should fit both the platform and your relationship. If someone replies with short messages, don't send them long paragraphs. Keep it brief, like, "Hey, saw your playlist, any tracks I should add to mine?" For emails or LinkedIn, one paragraph is enough to start. If they reply with interest, you can add more details.

Respect people's boundaries online. Not everyone checks their DMs all the time. Don't send multiple messages if they haven't replied; sending lots of "Did you see this?" texts can hurt your first impression. If you need to follow up after a day or two, keep it light: "Hey, just checking if you saw my message, if you're busy, no worries!" This shows you respect their time.

Don't assume you're close just because someone replies. If they only send an emoji or don't ask follow-up questions, take the hint and give them space. If the conversation is lively and they ask questions, match their energy. Don't get too personal or intense too soon; a little caution goes a long way online.

If you want to move the conversation to another platform, like from DM to a phone call or LinkedIn, suggest it gently: "Really enjoyed chatting here, would you like to connect on LinkedIn?" This keeps things low-pressure and makes it easy for them to say yes or no.

Set reminders so you don't forget to reply to someone who messaged you back. Keep track of your chats, and if the conversation faded but you want to reconnect, try, "Hey! Just realized our convo dropped off after [topic], how's everything going?" Thoughtful follow-ups show you care about keeping the connection going.

In the end, digital communication is about context and tone just as much as the words you use. Treat every DM like a real conversation, be curious, patient, and respectful. This makes it much easier to build real connections online.

The "Vibe Check" Method for Reading a Room or Group Chat

Walking into a room or joining a new group chat can feel like stepping onto a stage. You want to join in, but aren't sure how. This is where a "vibe check" helps: use your observation and instincts to sense the mood, see who's open to newcomers, and avoid awkward moments. In person, notice how people are grouped. Tight clusters with crossed arms and people facing inward usually mean a private conversation, so it's best to skip those. Open circles, relaxed body language, and eye contact are good signs that you can join in.

Look for signs of energy, like laughter, shared glances, or lively conversation. These usually mean the group is friendly and open to new people. If people copy each other's posture or lean in, it shows they're connected, but there might still be room for someone new, especially if someone is looking around or standing at the edge.

It's easy to spot low-energy groups: people slouching, looking at their phones, long silences, or one person talking while others seem distracted. These situations aren't always bad, but you might need to approach more gently or wait for a natural break. If you see someone on the edge of the group or looking around, they're probably open to a chat or would welcome an icebreaker.

A digital vibe check works much the same way. Instead of body language, pay attention to how fast and what kind of messages people send. If the chat is full of memes, GIFs, and quick replies, it's a lively group where you can jump in with a comment or question. If messages are rare, short, or just informational, it's better to wait and watch for a bit. Lots of emojis and reactions are like digital smiles; they show friendliness. On platforms like Discord or Slack, notice who replies quickly and who watches. If there are inside jokes, it's probably a close group, so start gently or mention what's already being discussed.

Timing matters as much as what you say. Ask yourself: Did someone make a joke? Has the mood changed? Is there a pause where you can join in naturally? In person, wait for a break or an opening in a group, then step in with a smile or a simple, "Mind if I jump in?" Making eye contact and getting a nod are good signs to join.

In chats, avoid barging in mid-thread unless it's a fast, moving, lively conversation; then it's okay to join with "Hey squad, quick question," or react with an emoji if you're nervous. Tagging someone by name is another subtle way to be noticed without interrupting the entire group.

The core of a vibe check is paying attention to context and flow, not waiting for formal permission. It's like surfing a wave: timing your entry so it feels natural. This practice helps you avoid awkwardness and makes it easier to blend in.

With a strong vibe, check skills, you'll slip into group conversations smoothly, appearing both welcoming and respectful of the group's flow. It also helps others feel more comfortable with you. Over time, you'll naturally sense when to speak up or hang back, no longer feeling out of place.

The key takeaway: reading the vibe matters just as much as finding the perfect words. It paves the way for smoother starts and fewer awkward moments. In the next chapter, you'll learn how to keep conversations going with confidence, so you won't freeze or run out of things to say when it counts.

Chapter Three

Overcoming Social Anxiety, Practical, Not Preachy

Micro-Challenges to Quiet Pre-Conversation Anxiety

Picture yourself waiting in line at a smoothie shop, scrolling through your phone while your heart races for no clear reason. You want to say something to the person next to you, like "love your shoes," or maybe give a nod and a smile, but you freeze. You start overthinking, imagine every possible outcome, and end up staying quiet.

Those nerves often get in the way of making small connections. Remember, most people are focused on themselves, not judging you, which can help ease your fear of rejection.

Your brain likes comfort and predictability. When you try something new, especially with people, your mind puts up warning signs to protect you from embarrassment or rejection. The way to get past this is to show your brain that social situations are safe by practicing gently and often until the fear fades. This is the idea behind exposure-based micro-challenges, a method supported by evidence-based therapy for social anxiety. Instead of jumping into big, scary events, you build confidence by taking small, intentional social risks. Each time you succeed, your brain learns that nothing bad happens when you reach out, even if it feels awkward.

Expanding your comfort zone is like stretching a muscle. If you avoid what makes you nervous, your comfort zone stays small. With steady, small steps, you start to feel more comfortable. Maybe you begin with eye contact and later work up to leading a meeting or asking someone out. The real value is in slowly building confidence, not just having one good conversation.

You don't need to make big gestures. Start as small as you want:

- Tomorrow morning, try to make brief eye contact and smile at your barista. There's no need to force a conversation.

- Next, compliment a coworker on something specific, like their clever idea or cool notebook. Notice their reaction, and your own.

- On another day, ask a stranger for the time, even if you already know it. The point isn't to get information, but to break the barrier in a low-risk way.

When the small tasks start to feel easier, try going alone to a Meetup or event for thirty minutes. Set a simple goal, like introducing yourself to one person or asking what brought them there. Leave whenever you want. The goal is to build confidence through small successes.

Some days will feel easier than others, and keeping track of your progress can help. Try making a simple "Social Challenge Tracker" on paper or your phone with three columns: Date, Challenge, and How It Felt/What Happened. Fill it out after each micro-challenge, even the small ones. Or, you can journal with the prompt: "What was easier than expected?" Often, worrying is worse than the real thing. Tracking helps you see your progress over time.

Social Challenge Tracker

Date Challenge Attempted: How It Felt/What Happened:

- 4/8 Smiled and made eye contact w/ barista. Nervous at first, but got a smile back

- 4/10 Complimented coworker's presentation. They looked surprised but happy.

- 4/12 Asked a stranger for directions. They were friendly; I felt a bit relieved.

- 4/15 Went to an art meetup solo. Talked to two people; left early but proud.

Recognize that setbacks happen and are part of the process. Embrace mistakes as learning opportunities to stay motivated and resilient.

To stay motivated and accountable, try having a buddy, like a friend or family member who gets it. After each micro-challenge, send them a quick text, like "Did it!" or "That was rough, but I tried." This keeps you connected, and they can cheer you on when you need it.

Set personal goals that work for you. If talking to strangers feels like too much, try holding eye contact a little longer. If big events seem overwhelming, join an online chat and send just one message. The goal is progress, not perfection.

Remember, your brain changes most when you experience small discomforts followed by relief; this is how new habits form. Each step into the unknown shows you that connection is possible and that anxiety doesn't have to win. Progress takes time, and every small effort counts.

Each micro-challenge is like dropping a pebble in a pond. As the ripples spread, those small actions build confidence. Over time, moments that once made you freeze will start to feel normal, showing you're not alone in this journey.

The "Awkward Turtle" Recovery Plan for Social Slip-Ups

Everyone sometimes stumbles over their words or makes mistakes. You might forget someone's name, interrupt to tell a story, laugh at the wrong time, spill a drink, or talk too loudly. These things happen to everyone, even confident people. Remember, social slip-ups are normal and show you're human, not alone in feeling embarrassed. A little humor can make mistakes feel smaller and more manageable.

For example, I've called coworkers by the wrong name and introduced myself to people I'd already met. It was awkward, but nothing bad happened. Most people are too busy thinking about their own mistakes to judge yours. Awkwardness is something everyone experiences. If you laugh it off, it becomes a funny story instead of something to feel ashamed about. People connect more with realness than with perfection.

My "awkward turtle" plan starts with a pause. When you feel flustered, stop, take a breath, and tell yourself, "That was clumsy." If you need to, say something light out loud, like "Classic me!" or "Sorry, my brain's on dial-up." A little humor shows you don't take yourself too seriously.

After you mention the awkward moment, switch to a new topic or ask a question. This helps get the conversation back on track and lets everyone move past the awkwardness.

If you interrupt someone, say, "Oops, got ahead of myself, what were you about to say?" If you forget a name, try, "Sorry, I blanked. Can you remind me of your name?" People value honesty over fake memory.

Lose your train of thought? Smile and say, "Ever start talking and forget where you were going? That just happened to me." Most find it relatable.

Keep a few recovery lines ready for when you blank out or make a mistake. If you interrupt someone, say, "Sorry, I got excited. Please finish." If you talk too much, try, "I'm rambling, your turn." If you laugh at the wrong time, say, "My timing's off!" In online meetings, you can use "Oops, talking on mute!" or "Tech gremlins." The goal is to move on and stay friendly.

Body language can help smooth things over after a mistake. The way you stand or sit says as much as your words. Try not to tense up or shrink away, since that shows embarrassment and can make others uncomfortable. Relax your shoulders, use open movements, and make friendly eye contact. Even a small, shy smile helps everyone feel at ease. Gestures like open hands or palms up show you're not hiding anything and that you're owning the mistake.

Often, the best thing you can do is let yourself move on. The main point is that people remember how you recover more than the mistake itself. A little humor and grace go a long way.

People tend to copy your attitude about mistakes. If you act relaxed, they will too. If you freeze up or apologize too much, it makes things tense. Just acknowledge the mistake, add a little humor, and move on.

Let's be honest: awkward moments are just part of being social. Nobody expects perfect conversation, and anyone who says otherwise isn't being honest. When you treat slip-ups as normal, they lose their power. Sometimes, those little stumbles make people remember you in a good way; they show you're real and relatable. "The awkward turtle" appears, tripping over words or drawing a blank, pause, add a hint of humor, then steer back on track with a gesture or question. Practice makes awkwardness less powerful.

How to Bounce Back After Being Ghosted or Ignored

You know the feeling: you send a thoughtful text, a funny meme, or a bold invite, and then nothing happens. Days go by. You keep checking your phone, rereading your last message, and wondering what went wrong.

Maybe you start doubting yourself, worrying you were too forward or said the wrong thing. It can feel like you've been erased.

Being ghosted or ignored hurts, especially when you've made an effort. It's hard whether it's a new friend, a group chat, a coworker, or someone you wanted to date. But this really happens to everyone, no matter how outgoing or put-together they seem.

People from all backgrounds have been ghosted or ignored. For example, a woman who moved to a new city reached out to a friend group but got no reply for weeks and felt invisible. A man in his thirties followed up with a coworker, but was left on read after they had chatted before. A nonbinary reader shared something in a group chat and felt exposed when no one replied. Stories like these are very common. Silence can feel personal, but most of the time, it's not about you.

Before you start blaming yourself, pause and look at the facts. People don't reply for all kinds of reasons, and it's rarely about your worth. Maybe they got busy, their phone died, they forgot, or something else came up. Maybe they're not ready for new connections or tough talks right now, or maybe ever. That doesn't mean you did anything wrong. Here's a quick self-checklist if you start to judge yourself: Did you send a lot of messages without waiting, or just one or two over a few days? Did you make demands or try to connect? Most of the time, you didn't "over-message", life just happened for them. Silence is neutral; it doesn't say anything about your value.

Remind yourself that people's silence usually has more to do with what's going on in their lives, like being overwhelmed, distracted, or in a certain mood, than with you. Try to stop those negative thoughts before they start. Instead of thinking, "I'm annoying," try, "They're busy," or "Maybe they're not in the mood to chat." It's not always easy, but it saves you a lot of emotional energy.

If you want to follow up for closure, clarity, or to try again, keep it relaxed and respectful. Avoid drama or guilt-tripping. For online conversations, a simple message like "Hey, just circling back in case my last message got lost!" shows you care without being pushy. If some time has passed, you can say, "No worries if you're busy, hope all is well!" This gives people a way out but lets them reply if they want. Sometimes, it helps to say directly, "If you're not interested, that's totally cool too." This is especially useful with new friends or dating, it's honest and makes things less awkward for everyone.

For in-person situations, if you said hi at work and didn't get much of a response, try not to read too much into it. Sometimes people are just shy or distracted. If you see them again, a simple "Hey again!" and a smile can reset things without any awkwardness. But if someone clearly doesn't want to talk, like no eye contact or only giving one-word answers, accept it kindly and focus your energy somewhere else.

It helps to step back and look at these moments differently. Instead of focusing on rejection, ask yourself, "What did I learn from this?" Maybe you notice you rush into connections, or you pick up on signals a bit late. Maybe you figure out which conversations make you feel good. Every ignored message is feedback, not about your worth, but about timing and fit.

Turn Setbacks Into Strength

After ghosting or silence, take five minutes to journal about what happened, stick to the facts ("I messaged Monday, no reply"). Ask: What feelings came up? What story did I tell myself? Is there another explanation for the silence? What did I learn about what I want from future connections? Finish with a self-affirmation: "Anyone else's reply doesn't define my value." Repeat as needed.

Being kind to yourself isn't just nice talk; it really changes how your brain handles these moments. When you treat yourself gently after social setbacks, it becomes easier to bounce back and try again. With practice, these moments help you build resilience and show you can handle disappointment and keep reaching out.

Connection isn't always guaranteed, but every time you risk being ignored and keep trying, you weaken the fear that silence means something is wrong with you. It proves that your effort matters more than any one reply. Each time you bounce back, your confidence grows, and the next attempt feels less scary and more doable.

Turning Social Fear Of Missing Out (FOMO) Into Connection Opportunities

FOMO is that feeling in your chest when you see photos of friends at a concert, notice coworkers laughing together, or watch a group chat making plans you weren't invited to. At its core, FOMO isn't just about wanting to be everywhere; it's a sign that you want connection and belonging. Social anxiety and FOMO often go hand in hand, creating a cycle. Fear of missing out grows when you hold back from reaching out, and anxiety rises as you picture everyone else bonding without you. Deep down, it's a normal desire to feel included and valued. That longing is human, not something to hide.

FOMO's roots are emotional, woven into our brains for survival. We're wired to fear exclusion because, long ago, being left out could mean real danger. Now, it just means aching for messages that don't arrive or feeling invisible when others make plans. It's easy to slip into comparison mode, believing everyone else has a full calendar or a thriving social life while you're stuck on the sidelines. But that ache can also be useful; it points straight to what you want: more moments of connection.

Instead of letting FOMO drag you down, treat it like a compass. When those pangs hit, pause and ask yourself: what exactly am I wishing for? Is it the sense of being known in a regular group, the excitement of trying something new, or simply the comfort of having someone to talk to on a weekend? Track your patterns. Notice which people, events, or online communities keep sparking that sense of longing. Maybe you always feel left out seeing photos from trivia nights at a local bar, or maybe your heart tugs when coworkers organize a lunch, and you're not included. These recurring moments are clues; they show where you want to belong.

Make a list, yes, actually write it down, of groups or events that catch your interest, even if they seem intimidating. Scan community boards, meetup apps, or even friends' Instagram stories for ideas. Don't focus on the ones so exclusive they stress you out; look for approachable spaces that welcome new faces. Maybe it's a volunteer night at the library, an open mic at a coffee shop, or an online book club. If big crowds feel too much, look for smaller gatherings or digital spaces where you can dip your toe in before fully jumping in.

Once you spot a few possibilities, the next step is to shift FOMO into action with gentle entry points. You don't need to plunge into the center of the action right away. One easy strategy: offer to help out at an event. Volunteering gives you an instant reason to talk to people; passing out programs, setting up chairs, or helping run a game makes you part of the team from the start. If that's not your speed, send a low-pressure DM to someone in the group whose interests overlap with yours. You could say, "Hey, I noticed you posted about hiking trails. Do you have any favorites for beginners?" That single message opens a door without demanding instant friendship.

Suggesting low-key hangouts is another smooth way in. Instead of waiting for others to invite you (which only fuels FOMO), take a small risk: "I'm grabbing coffee Saturday if anyone wants to join," or "Game night at my place Friday, open invite!" Not everyone will jump at the chance, but those who do are signaling interest in connecting with you. Even if only one person responds, that's one more link than before. These gentle nudges show initiative without pressure.

The hardest part of all this is keeping your focus on what you can do rather than what you're missing. It's natural for your brain to replay every missed invite or scroll through endless highlight reels online. But comparison is a trap; nobody is everywhere or included in everything, no matter how it looks on social media. An important mindset shift: "You don't have to be everywhere to belong somewhere." Repeat this whenever FOMO flares up. Belonging is about building meaningful bonds in places where you feel comfortable. Celebrate each small step toward new connections, a reply to your DM, showing up at an event for twenty minutes, or introducing yourself to one new person.

Affirmations can help rewire your thinking over time. Try these on days when FOMO hits hardest: "My calendar doesn't define my worth," "It's okay to start small," and "Every effort counts." Write them on sticky notes or set reminders on your phone if that helps keep them top of mind.

FOMO loses its grip when you use it as fuel, not proof that you're left out forever, but as motivation to move toward what matters most to you. Instead of letting envy or regret keep you stuck, channel your energy into action; even tiny ones count.

As this chapter closes, remember: social anxiety and FOMO might always pop up from time to time, but they don't have to shut you out from connection. Each small step transforms longing into belonging and shows you're capable of shaping your social life in real ways. Next up: we'll dig deeper into group dynamics and how to find your way into conversations, no matter how intimidating they seem at first.

Chapter Four

Group Dynamics and Seamless Entry Points

How to Join a Group Conversation Without Interrupting

Imagine you're at the edge of a birthday party, wanting to join a lively group but feeling a bit awkward. Most people have felt left out at some point, hoping for a sign that it's okay to join in. Group conversations have their own rhythms and signals. If you learn to notice these cues, you'll start to see opportunities to join almost anywhere.

Group conversations aren't like one-on-one chats. There are more voices, and the energy shifts around. Pay attention to see if a group is open or closed. The easiest way to tell is by watching body language. Open groups usually form loose circles or U-shapes, with people facing outward, leaving gaps, moving their feet, and keeping their arms relaxed. These signs mean they're open to others joining. Closed groups stand close together, face inward, cross their arms, and avoid looking around. If a group seems closed, don't take it personally. They might be deep in conversation or sharing something private. It's better to wait for a more open group than to try to force your way in.

Along with body language, listen for other signals. If you hear laughter or notice a pause, the group might be switching topics; these are good times to join. Laughter can open the door for a moment. Pauses after jokes or strong reactions are also good chances to step in. But if everyone is focused on one person telling a story, wait until they're done before joining.

When you see a good moment, don't make a big entrance. Try the "hover and listen" approach. Stand near enough to be noticed, but not so close that you interrupt. Keep your arms relaxed and your hands visible to people. If you catch someone's eye, give a small smile or nod to show you're friendly. Often, just being there encourages someone to make space for you.

Eye contact can be a quiet but strong signal. If you meet someone's eyes and they smile, that's often an invitation to join. Wait for a natural pause, then step in calmly. You can say, "Mind if I join?" or "That sounds funny, what happened?" These simple phrases show you respect the group and aren't trying to take over.

If you didn't hear the whole conversation, be honest about it. Saying, "I just caught the last part, were you talking about [topic]?" Shows sincerity and helps you connect genuinely with others.

You don't need to be the center of attention to add value. Share something real, a quick thought, a personal story, or a follow-up question. If the group is talking about last night's game, give your opinion or ask what they think. If they're sharing pet stories, mention something funny your cat does. Keep your first comment short and let others join in too.

Sometimes joining a group doesn't work out. Maybe the group stays closed, avoids eye contact, or the conversation stops. This happens to everyone, even people who are great at socializing. Don't let it bother you. It's usually just a matter of timing or the group's mood. Leave smoothly by saying, "I'll catch up later!" or giving a quick nod before moving on. Handling these moments well shows you have good social skills, not that you've failed.

Think Back

After your next social event, take a moment to jot down:

- What body language did I observe before joining?

- Did I wait for the right pause or laugh?

- How did I introduce myself or contribute?

- Did the group feel open or closed, and why?

- If my entry didn't work, how did I exit and feel?

Thinking about these questions helps you notice patterns. With practice, spotting group signals will become natural.

Every time you try, you're practicing. Look for open circles, use laughter as a sign, or leave politely when needed. Each attempt helps you get better at joining group conversations.

"Vibe Checks" in Action, Group Energy

Think of a high-energy group where everyone's laughing too loud, interrupting with side jokes, finishing each other's stories, and somehow having three conversations at once. It's messy, fast, and ridiculously fun, like the room's running on caffeine, inside jokes, and zero chill.

Other groups are quieter and more organized. People take turns, speak softly, and stay on one topic. In these groups, lower your energy, keep your comments short, and wait for a story to end or for laughter before you speak. If the group isn't joking around, avoid loud jokes. Try to match their pace and volume.

Inside jokes show that the group is close. If you don't understand the joke, don't pretend to laugh. Just smile, listen, and wait until the conversation moves to a topic you can join. Avoid interrupting these moments.

Online groups have their own ways of communicating. Pay attention to how people interact on Discord or WhatsApp. Is the chat full of memes and GIFs, or do people write in full sentences and keep things formal? Before you join in, watch how others talk. In fast, meme-heavy chats, start by reacting to posts or sharing a meme that fits. In more serious groups, keep your replies focused and wait for quiet moments to bring up new topics. Notice how people use emojis; lots of them usually mean a relaxed vibe, while just a few suggest a more serious tone. Adjusting to these signals helps you fit in faster.

Most importantly, respect the group's boundaries. Every group has unspoken rules. If people are sharing old stories you can't join, listen until the topic becomes more general. If someone is doing most of the talking, wait for them to invite you in before speaking. When the mood gets serious or emotions run high, it's best to wait and watch until things calm down.

Making Friends in New Cities or Situations

Moving to a new city or starting a new job can feel overwhelming, but making new friends starts with small steps and a bit of effort. Look for events where people are open to meeting newcomers. Meetup, Eventbrite, Discord, or Facebook events are good places to find groups based on your interests. Pick something that sounds interesting, even if you're only a little curious. For online meetups, you can join in and get to know people without the pressure of being in the same room.

After you find an event or group chat, try using mutual contacts to get introduced. Ask coworkers or neighbors about their social circles; most people are happy to make introductions. After an event, send a message to someone about something you talked about, like, "Want to check out that trail this weekend?" Simple invites like coffee or lunch help turn acquaintances into friends.

Language and cultural differences can make things harder. International student events or language exchanges are helpful because everyone there is looking to connect. If you're unsure, online spaces can feel less intimidating and let you message people without the stress of meeting face-to-face.

Small challenges help build your confidence. Try going to one new group event each month, introduce yourself to two people, and follow up afterward. These small steps help you make connections and feel less pressure each time.

The Art of Noticing Outsiders, and Drawing Them In

In every group, there's usually someone who stays quiet or sits off to the side. Maybe you've felt that way before. You can spot outsiders by noticing who doesn't talk much, sits on the edge, or seems a bit disconnected. Being aware of this helps you include others.

Invite quieter people to join in without making them feel uncomfortable. Ask open questions like, "What do you think?" or refer to something they said earlier: "I liked what [Name] said about that project, want to share more?" You can also make space next to you or use eye contact to show they're welcome.

Online, you can tag new people in group chats or send them a quick message like, "Welcome! Let me know if you have questions." Combining a public welcome with private support helps people feel like they belong more quickly.

People remember when someone included them. These small moments build trust and loyalty. Many people can recall a single invite to coffee or a chat that made a big difference.

Being inclusive isn't just a nice extra; it makes groups stronger. Welcoming everyone leads to better conversations, closer friendships, and makes sure no one feels left out.

When you include others, you turn closed groups into open ones, making everyone feel like they belong.

If you're unsure how to start, try these sample lines in digital spaces:

- "Hey [Name], what's your take on this?"

- "I noticed you're new, welcome! Feel free to jump in or DM me if you want."

- "Good point earlier, [Name]. Want to elaborate for the group?"

You can also move your chair or turn your body to invite someone into your group. These small gestures add up and can really change how people feel around you.

Being inclusive isn't about making big speeches. It's about noticing who's left out and inviting them in gently. Sometimes it's as simple as remembering someone's name or bringing up their idea if it was missed. You don't have to be the leader or the most outgoing person; often, the quietest people are best at noticing who needs a little encouragement.

In any setting, office meetings, family dinners, or online groups, you can build trust just by reaching out to people on the edge. You might be surprised how often these small moments lead to lasting connections.

To wrap up, remember that every group has space for one more person. Noticing who feels left out and including them can turn an ordinary get-together into something special. Strong groups are built on small acts of empathy. As you move forward, watch for these moments; you never know whose day or life you might change with a simple invitation. Next, we'll explore how listening and empathy can deepen your conversations.

Chapter Five

Moving Beyond Small Talk

How to Shift From Small Talk to Real Talk

You know that moment at a barbecue or in the break room when the conversation runs out of steam? Maybe you've already talked about the weather, work, or traffic, and now you're both looking at your drinks or checking your phones, hoping for something more interesting. Small talk is often necessary, but it rarely stands out. The best conversations happen when you move past the basics and talk about what matters to you, but making that shift can feel tricky without some help. I call these moments' transition triggers', quick cues or signals that help move from casual chat to a real connection.

To spot these triggers, pay close attention to your conversation partner's energy and interest. Notice when their eyes light up, their voice gets more animated, or they lean in a bit. Maybe you mention a band, and they start telling you about their first concert. Or you ask about their weekend, and they smile as they talk about hiking with their dog. That means you've found a topic that matters to them. This is your chance to move beyond small talk. You don't have to be smooth or pushy. Notice when someone gets excited and ask them to share more. On the other hand, if the conversation feels slow or you get short answers and distracted looks, that's a sign to change topics or end the chat politely.

Moving from small talk to real conversation is easier than most people think. The trick is to use bridge phrases that sound natural and show real interest, not like you're grilling someone. If someone says they're new in town, ask, "What brought you here?" instead of just nodding. When jobs come up, skip the usual "What do you do?" and try, "How did you end up in that field?" or "Is it what you always hoped for?" These kinds of questions invite stories and show you care. Good transitions sound like, "That's fascinating, I haven't met anyone who does that. How did you get started?" or "You said you love traveling; was there a destination that shaped your perspective?" These gentle prompts let people know it's okay to open up.

Context can help you move conversations deeper. Use what's happening around you to start more interesting topics. At a music festival, you could say, "This place has such a cool vibe. Have you been to anything like this before?" If you're stuck waiting for a delayed flight, instead of complaining about the airline again, try, "Is this your first time going to [destination]?" or "What's the most random travel story you have?" Even at work, let the situation help: "It's interesting how everyone here comes from different backgrounds. What led you into this industry?" If someone brings up a sport or hobby, follow up: "Soccer always looks fun but intense. Did you play as a kid or start later?"

It's useful to know when someone is open to a deeper conversation and when it's better to keep things light. Signs like relaxed posture, open gestures, steady eye contact, and real laughter mean they're interested. If they put their phone away or forget about their drink, they're probably engaged. Sometimes people even copy your body language when they feel comfortable. But if you see crossed arms, short answers, or lots of glances around the room or at their watch, it's not the right time for deeper topics. Some places, like crowded bars or quick elevator rides, aren't great for meaningful talks either. Save personal questions for quieter times or one-on-one moments when people feel more at ease.

Spotting Green Lights for Real Talk

- Their eyes brighten, or their voice picks up when discussing certain topics

- They ask follow-up questions or share personal anecdotes

- They make steady eye contact and relax their posture

- Laughter feels easy and genuine

- They set aside distractions (phone, bag, food)

- The setting feels chill (coffee shop corner, park bench, not mid-chaos)

If you spot one or more of these signs, it's usually a good time to move past small talk. If not, keep things light until the mood changes.

You don't have to pry or put on an act. Just notice these small signals and respond with real curiosity. Sometimes one thoughtful question is enough to start a real conversation where both people feel understood. If it doesn't work, that's okay; you can always go back to lighter topics until another chance comes up.

The Power of "Tell Me More", Prompting Deeper Stories

Just saying "tell me more" can open up a conversation in new ways. Whether you're at a party, in a café, or on a video call, inviting someone to share more can turn small talk into a real story. When you say "tell me more," it shows you're genuinely interested. It's not pushy, it just gives the other person a chance to share what they want. It might feel a bit awkward at first, but most people like talking about things that matter to them.

The key is to use "tell me more" as a gentle follow-up, not to put someone on the spot. If someone says they went camping, don't fire off a bunch of questions. Instead, try, "That sounds like an adventure, tell me more about where you went." This lets them share the details they want, maybe about the view or a funny story. You're inviting them to share, not just give facts. Sometimes people give short answers, and that's okay; some need more time to open up or aren't in the mood. It's fine to move on or try again later.

Think of follow-up questions as steps that help the conversation grow. Start with "tell me more," and listen for details that stand out. If they say it rained the whole time, you could ask, "What was that like for you?" or "Did the weather change your plans?" Maybe they'll talk about building tarp shelters or playing board games at night, and you can ask, "What happened next?" These questions keep the chat going and show you care. The goal is to be curious about their experience, not just the facts, without being pushy.

Giving feedback as you listen helps keep the conversation friendly and natural. Nodding, showing excitement, and saying things like "Really?" or "That's wild!" let the other person know you're engaged. If their story gets personal or emotional, you don't need the perfect reply. Just say, "Wow, that sounds intense," or repeat something they said, like, "So you spent all night searching for your tent in the rain?" to show you're listening. Your body language matters too. Lean in, make eye contact, and put your phone away to show you're paying attention.

Here are some quick script ideas for practicing this in real scenarios:

Everyday Script & Scenarios

At a friend's party, someone says, "I've gotten really into hiking this year." Instead of a simple nod, try, "You said you love hiking, what's your favorite trail?" They might tell you about a hidden waterfall or a muddy mishap.

At work, when a colleague mentions their team finished a unique project, you could say, "Your project sounds unique. How did your team approach it?" They might share insights from their brainstorming sessions or challenges they faced.

On a date, if someone says they moved across the country last year, build on it: "You mentioned you moved here for a reason. What drew you in?" This opens the door for them to talk about their motivations, whether it's a job, an adventure, or being closer to family.

Questions like "tell me more," "what was that like?" or "How did that go?" let the other person decide how deep to go, while helping you build a real connection.

Try Using "Tell Me More" in Everyday Chats

Scenario 1 – Social:

Cookout conversation. Someone says, "I finally started learning guitar."

You: "That's awesome, tell me more! What made you want to pick it up?"

Scenario 2 – Work:

At lunch, a coworker says, "Our team's been working on this wild new app."

You: "That sounds ambitious! What's different about your approach?"

Scenario 3 – Dating:

They mention, "I used to live abroad."

You: "No way! Where did you live, and what was the wildest part about adapting?"

Try saying these lines out loud. They might feel awkward at first, but they'll grow more natural with practice.

In the end, "tell me more" is about being real, not just filling time with small talk. When people feel welcome to share what matters to them, conversations become meaningful and memorable for both of you.

Vulnerability, Boundaries, and When to "Go Deep"

Most people want real connections, but moving past small talk takes a bit of vulnerability. In conversation, this means showing a little of your true self. It's about sharing a real moment, not just swapping headlines. You don't need to tell your whole life story to a stranger or get too personal at a networking event. Instead, try sharing a thought or feeling to see if the other person does the same. The right amount of openness makes conversations deeper, but too much can feel uncomfortable.

Meaningful conversations often begin when someone takes a small risk, like saying they get nervous at big events or are still learning a new job. These aren't big confessions, just small ways to invite connection. For example, saying, "Networking always makes me a bit jittery, does it get easier?" or "I'm new in town and still looking for good late-night food, any tips?" shows you're open and gives others a chance to relate. If the other person responds with understanding or shares something too, it's a sign you can go a bit deeper. If they change the subject or seem uneasy, it's best to keep things light.

Trying small, honest comments helps you avoid going too deep too quickly. It's like dipping your toe in before jumping into a pool. You're not asking for someone's biggest secrets, just looking for shared experiences or feelings. Even saying, "I always feel a bit awkward at parties, does that happen to you?" gives the other person a chance to connect or keep things light if they want.

It's normal to worry about sharing too much or getting into sensitive topics. That's where boundaries come in, those invisible lines that keep conversations comfortable. Boundaries depend on the person, the situation, and the culture. Some people trust quickly, while others take time to trust. Some places, like work events or large groups, aren't the right setting for personal topics. If you're not sure, let the other person set the pace.

If you see signs that someone is uncomfortable, like breaking eye contact, getting tense, or giving short answers, it's good to acknowledge it. Saying, "No worries if that's not something you want to talk about," gives them an easy way out without any awkwardness. If you notice you've shared too much, you can say, "Sorry if I went a bit far; sometimes I forget not everyone wants my life story." A little humor can help make things comfortable again.

Understanding boundaries is just as important as knowing what to share. Culture and context matter; a group of friends might be open about feelings, while others aren't. In professional or formal settings, keep things light unless you know the person well. In casual settings, you can be a bit more open, but not every topic fits. If you're unsure, watch for signs like distraction, short answers, or someone moving away. That's your cue to change the subject.

If you notice discomfort in yourself or the other person, don't push for deeper conversation. Instead, switch back to a neutral topic, something about your surroundings, or a safe current event. For example, "This playlist's pretty good, do you know who picks the music here?" or "It's surprising how packed it gets on Fridays" are easy ways to change the subject. You can also go back to earlier topics or shared interests.

If someone starts sharing something heavy and you're not ready for that level of conversation or don't have the energy, kindly set your own boundary. You can say, "Thanks for trusting me with that. I'm not sure I have the best advice, but I can listen," or "That sounds tough. I hope you have support." This way, you're being supportive without taking on too much.

Handling vulnerability and boundaries isn't about following strict rules. It's about paying attention to words, tone, and body language. Build trust by taking small risks in conversation and adjusting if things get tense. You don't have to share everything with everyone. Notice when it feels safe to go deeper. When you find the right balance, those conversations often stay with you.

Steering Chats Toward Shared Interests

Think of every conversation as a map with different paths. Some end quickly, while others lead to interesting topics you both enjoy. 'Conversation maps' aren't just a metaphor; they're a helpful way to guide small talk toward more engaging moments. Each topic is like a branch, leading to new directions with every shared story or fact. You might start with "How's your week?" and end up talking about movies, travel, or a unique hobby. Seeing conversations this way makes it easier to spot good topics and choose the best direction.

You don't have to be an expert to use this approach. Sometimes I make quick mind maps before social events or sketch out ideas for work meetings. On paper or in your head, start with general topics like "work," "weekend," or "music," then think of possible branches. If someone mentions they love climbing, you could talk about outdoor sports, travel, or even funny injuries. If one topic doesn't go anywhere, try another. This kind of planning might seem a bit nerdy, but it helps you feel more confident and keeps conversations interesting.

The main thing is to listen for hooks, small details, or side comments that hint at shared interests. Hooks can be anything: someone mentioning a favorite show, loving spicy food, or having a dog named Loki. Even tiny details can lead to new topics. Your job is to notice these openings. If someone talks about a book, a game, or a unique hobby, that's a chance to connect on a deeper level.

When you spot a hook, guide the conversation toward that topic with real interest. You don't need to make a big shift; follow up naturally. If you both watch the same show, ask, "You're a fan too? What did you think of season two's twist?" If someone visited Thailand, say, "That's on my bucket list. Was anything about it unexpected?" Ask specific follow-up questions to find common ground. Even if you haven't had the same experience, show genuine curiosity: "Surfing looks both scary and exciting. Is it as tough as it seems?" Share your own stories or ask open-ended questions to keep the conversation going.

Not every conversation will reveal a shared interest right away. Sometimes people give short answers or miss your hints. If that happens, don't worry, try a different topic. For example, "You mentioned sci-fi books, do you have a favorite author?" If things still don't pick up, it's okay to end the chat politely: "It's been nice talking; let's catch up again soon!" If someone shares something interesting but doesn't want to go deeper, thank them and move on: "Thanks for the podcast tip, I'll check it out." Keep things friendly for next time.

We've all been trapped repeating surface-level topics, like the weather, for the third time. That's when your mental map is a lifesaver. If a group is focused on something you're not into, use humor or curiosity: "I'll admit I'm clueless about football, but what makes it so fun to watch?" Or casually pivot: "Speaking of teams, has anyone tried an escape room?" This lets others bring their interests and can refresh the energy.

Maps often intersect in unexpected spots. I once talked with someone deeply into cosplay and anime conventions, both of which were out of my wheelhouse. But when she mentioned making her own costumes, I got curious about her creative process. This led to an in-depth conversation on art and self-expression, an intersection I would've missed if I'd focused only on my own interests.

Use Conversation Mapping

Next time you're prepping for an event or want to improve your chats, try this:

- On paper or in your head, list three general topics likely to come up: work, travel, and entertainment.

- For each, brainstorm two or three possible branches (under travel: favorite places, biggest mishaps, dream trips).

- During conversations, listen for hooks and see which branches seem lively. If one stalls, try another route from your map.

This method isn't about scripting every word; it's about staying flexible and letting each chat naturally lead. The more you practice noticing hooks and steering toward shared interests, the smoother and more rewarding your interactions become.

To wrap up: meaningful conversations aren't luck, they're created by those who watch for cues and aren't afraid to try new conversational roads. With your conversation map ready, finding genuine points of connection becomes much easier. Up next: how effective listening helps all these conversational branches reach even richer destinations.

Chapter Six

Active Listening and Genuine Empathy

The "Echo Technique" for Instant Rapport

Have you ever met someone who really makes you feel heard and understood? It's not magic; they're usually just using simple habits that show they care. One of the best is the "Echo Technique." When someone repeats a word or phrase you used, maybe adding a follow-up question, you feel noticed and valued right away. That's how instant rapport happens.

The Echo Technique is all about repeating back the other person's words. You pick up on a phrase, feeling, or detail they mention and use it in your reply. Psychologists call this mirroring or verbal validation, and it feels good because our brains like hearing our own words echoed. Babies do this with caregivers, and adults react the same way. It helps us trust others and open up. You can use this technique anywhere, from job interviews to casual conversations.

It's not about copying people word-for-word; that gets awkward fast. The trick is to echo with real curiosity. For example, if someone says, "I just moved here from Austin," you could reply, "You moved here recently?

How's the city treating you?" Or if they mention, "I'm into improv comedy," you might say, "Improv? That sounds fun! How did you get into it?" You're picking out one detail and building on it, which shows you're truly listening and encourages them to share more.

Sometimes, echoing someone's feelings works better than repeating facts. If a person says, "Work's been overwhelming lately," don't jump in with advice. Instead, reflect their emotion: "Sounds like it's been a lot to handle." This kind of response shows empathy and helps people feel understood. If they share good news, like "I finally finished my portfolio!", match their excitement: "That's awesome! You must be relieved." Echoing emotions like this helps build stronger connections and makes you someone people enjoy talking to.

It's important to use the echo technique thoughtfully. To avoid sounding repetitive or distracted, echo when you notice something important, then follow up with open-ended questions or a quick personal reaction. For example, if someone says, "I'm a designer," you could reply, "A designer? Interesting! What projects do you work on?" Echoing "designer" invites them to share more and shows you're interested, helping your conversation feel natural and engaging.

Echoing can also help clear up details and keep the conversation moving. If a friend says, "I'm running a half-marathon next month," you might reply, "A half-marathon? Wow! Have you run races before?" You're not grilling them; it just shows you remembered what they said and are inviting them to share more if they want.

How you echo is just as important as what you say. Match your tone to their mood. If they're being vulnerable, keep your voice gentle. If they're excited, show some energy too. Try not to sound robotic, like saying, "You said improv. How did you get into improv?" Instead, let your words come naturally from real curiosity.

Practice an Echo Technique in Real Life

Give it a try this week. Listen to a podcast or YouTube interview where people are having a real conversation. Write down three phrases that stand out. Notice how a good host echoes words or feelings to help the guest open up.

Next, try this in three real-life conversations this week, at work, with friends, or even at the gym. Listen for a detail or emotion, and echo it back in your reply. For example:

- "You started bouldering, that's intense! What got you into it?"

- "Your family lives out of state? That must make holidays interesting."

- "You said the new boss is strict, how's that changing your work?"

If practicing active listening feels awkward at first, don't worry-it's normal. Echoing gets easier with consistent practice. After each conversation, reflect on what felt natural and what didn't. Notice how people react; often, they'll open up and seem more engaged when they feel you're truly listening. Building this habit gradually will boost your confidence and make your interactions more meaningful over time.

Getting good at this simple habit can really improve your relationships, both at work and in your personal life. People want to feel heard, and when you reflect their words with real curiosity, you become more memorable and build trust. Even shy people open up when they feel truly listened to. Echoing isn't about talking more; it's about listening better and making others feel valued.

Decoding Micro-Expressions and Subtle Body Language

Understanding how someone really feels is about more than just their words. Most communication happens through micro-expressions and subtle body language. You've probably noticed when someone is excited, bored, or annoyed, even if they don't say it. Micro-expressions are quick facial cues that show what someone is feeling, sometimes before they even realize it. These are universal; studies show that people everywhere have similar expressions of surprise, skepticism, discomfort, and genuine enjoyment. They happen fast, but once you know what to look for, you'll start spotting emotions others might miss.

For example, surprise shows up as lifted eyebrows, wide eyes, and an open mouth, but only for a moment. If you notice this while talking, you've probably surprised the person. Skepticism can look like one eyebrow raised, lips pressed together, or a slow blink; all of these show doubt. Discomfort might show as a tight-lipped smile, a clenched jaw, or someone looking away often. Real enjoyment is easy to spot in relaxed, crinkling eyes (those "crow's feet") and a big, genuine smile. Watching for these reactions helps you understand what people are really feeling.

With practice, you can get better at noticing these quick signals. Start simple: raised eyebrows usually mean interest or surprise, and a tight-lipped smile often shows someone feels unsure or uncomfortable. It's that polite but awkward grin that says, "I'm not sure." Leaning in means someone is interested, while crossed arms can hint at defensiveness or discomfort. But remember, context matters; not every crossed arm is negative. Sometimes people are just cold or don't know where to put their hands. Look for patterns: if someone leans back, folds their arms, and avoids eye contact, they're probably closing off.

You don't need to read minds; pick up enough nonverbal cues to sense the mood. Sometimes people say "I'm fine," but their body language tells a different story: maybe a forced smile, stiff posture, or fidgety feet. If you notice these mismatches, don't worry. Use them as signs to adjust. If someone looks uneasy, maybe you hit a sensitive topic or your joke didn't land. You can acknowledge it and gently change the subject: "Seems like that's a sensitive topic, want to talk about something else?" On the other hand, if you see real smiles and bright eyes, you're probably on the right track and can keep going with more energy.

Practicing these skills can actually be fun. Try watching videos, TikToks, YouTube clips, or reality TV with the sound off, and guess what people are feeling based on their expressions and body language. Pause at key moments and write down your best guess, maybe amusement, awkwardness, surprise, or irritation. Then watch again with sound to see how close you were. Doing this often will help you get better at spotting micro-expressions in real life. You can try this with commercials, movies, or even during video calls, and watch people's faces when someone else is talking.

The Micro-Expression Challenge

Choose five brief TikToks or reels (thirty seconds or less). Watch each video without sound, pausing 3 times per video. At each pause, identify the emotion on the main person's face, pleasure, skepticism, surprise, or annoyance, based on their eyebrows, smiles (real or forced), eyes, and posture. When you finish, watch the videos again with audio to see how your interpretations compare with the actual mood. Afterward, reflect on which cues were easiest or most challenging to notice.

When you're talking to someone, paying attention to their body language helps you be more flexible and empathetic. If they light up, lean in, have bright eyes, ask more questions, or follow up, you've found a topic they enjoy. If their posture shrinks or their arms fold tighter, don't ignore it, try switching to a lighter topic or acknowledge how they feel: "Seems like this topic is a bit heavy, want to move on?" Adjusting like this shows you care and helps people feel safe and respected.

Cultural differences and personal habits can affect body language, so stay open to the little things. Still, once you start noticing, most signals are pretty consistent. By picking up on micro-expressions and small changes, you'll become a better communicator, avoid misunderstandings, and build stronger, more meaningful relationships where people feel truly seen and understood.

Listening With Your Whole Self, Not Just Your Ears

It's surprising how many people think listening is just about hearing words. You probably know that feeling when you're talking, and someone is nodding, but their eyes are on their phone or looking past you. Suddenly, you feel invisible, like you're talking to a wall. That's the difference between someone who's just hearing and someone who's really listening with their whole self. Whole-self listening means being fully present, using your ears, eyes, mind, and body. You're not just hearing words; you're giving your full attention and making the other person feel important. This is what helps people open up, trust you, and want to keep talking.

Passive nodding is a classic fake; it happens in meetings, classes, on dates, everywhere. You see someone nodding or saying "mm-hmm," but their mind is somewhere else. Real, intentional listening feels different for both people. When you're truly present, you lean in a bit, your face shows interest, and your eyes stay focused, not jumping to your phone or looking around. You're not planning your reply or checking the time; you're right there in the moment. It's a full-body experience. When someone gives you that kind of attention, it feels magnetic and makes you want to share more.

Distractions are everywhere, phones buzz, laptops chime, and group chats ping all day. To really pay attention, you have to be intentional about removing distractions. The quickest way is to put your phone out of sight and set it to silent. I usually put mine in a bag or pocket, so I'm not tempted. In person, turn your body toward the speaker, with your shoulders and knees facing them. These small changes show, "You have my attention." On video calls, close any tabs you don't need. It's easy to get distracted by email or TikTok and miss something important. Even one notification can break your focus and make the other person feel unimportant.

Body language is a big part of whole-self listening. The right signals can make someone feel noticed, while the wrong ones can shut things down quickly. A small head tilt is one of my favorites; it shows curiosity without words. Leaning in a bit (without crowding) shows you care about what's being said. Matching someone's posture helps, too. If they're relaxed, mirror that energy, but don't copy them exactly; it just helps them feel at ease. Your face should match the mood of the conversation. If they share something happy, let your eyes soften and smile naturally. If they talk about something tough, let your expression show empathy, don't force it, but don't hide it either.

Eye contact can be tricky for some people; it can feel intense or awkward if you make too much of it. The trick is to aim for comfortable eye contact about two-thirds of the time, and look away naturally so you're not staring. If I notice someone getting uncomfortable, I glance away for a moment (maybe at my coffee or the table), then look back. This keeps things feeling natural and not awkward.

If your focus slips and your mind drifts to dinner or tomorrow's deadlines, notice it and gently bring your attention back to the speaker. Don't be hard on yourself; everyone's mind wanders, especially during long conversations or meetings. The important thing is to notice when it happens and return to the present.

If you want to improve, try having a five-minute conversation with someone you trust, without interrupting or checking your phone. Set a timer and listen, no advice, no fixing, no planning your next response. Notice how much more connected you feel afterward. Another tip is to do a quick mindfulness check before an important talk: take three slow breaths and remind yourself to stay present. These small habits add up quickly.

Staying physically still is powerful too; fidgeting can signal boredom or impatience, even if you don't mean it. Try to keep your body calm, with your feet on the ground and hands relaxed (not tapping or scrolling). After the conversation, take a moment to reflect: Did you feel more engaged? Did the other person open up more than usual? Thinking about this helps you figure out what works best for you.

Whole-self listening isn't about being perfect; it's about making people feel important during the time you're with them. You can't do this all day, every day; it takes effort. But when you choose to be fully present, even short conversations can be memorable. People notice when you really show up for them, not just with your ears but with your whole presence, and they remember how it felt long after the conversation ends.

Responding to One-Word Answers Without Feeling Shut Down

Everyone knows that awkward moment when you ask someone how they're doing or what's new, and they say "Fine," "Yeah," or "Nope." It can feel like you've hit a wall, and it's easy to wonder if you did something wrong. But these short replies usually don't mean you failed or that the person doesn't like you. One-word answers happen for lots of reasons, maybe the person is tired, distracted, shy, or just not in the mood to talk. Maybe they had a rough day or don't know what to say. These moments can sting, but they don't mean you're bad at conversation.

It's easy to take short answers personally, especially if you already feel nervous. You might want to give up or go quiet, but before you decide the conversation is awkward, pause and take a breath. The key isn't to push harder, but to respond with empathy and curiosity. Instead of asking more questions or forcing the topic, try gently building on what they said. For example, if someone says, "It was okay" about their weekend, you could ask, "What made it just 'okay'?" This shows you noticed their mood and gives them a chance to share more. If that doesn't work, try a related but easier topic: "Anything else going on this week?" Sometimes a gentle change works better than digging deeper.

If someone seems really closed off, avoids eye contact, or shows with their body language that they want to be left alone, acknowledge it gently: "Long day?" or "You seem tired." This gives them a chance to share or feel seen. If they still don't open up, that's fine; you've respected their boundaries. Offer a kind way out instead of pushing: "Would you rather talk about something else?" or "No pressure, I'll let you decompress, and we can catch up later." Sometimes, giving space is the best thing you can do.

Context matters, too; people give one-word answers for lots of reasons. Maybe the timing is off, they're distracted, or the setting isn't right. Some people are just quiet or need time to warm up. Notice things like the environment, time of day, and who else is around. For example, group settings can make some people go quiet, and a loud or busy place can make even talkative people give short replies. Paying attention to the situation helps you decide whether to keep trying or step back.

Knowing when to follow up, change the subject, or pause takes practice. If someone seems open but isn't sure what to say, a gentle follow-up like, "Was it one of those weekends where nothing went as planned?" can help. If they seem checked out, only giving yes/no answers or avoiding eye contact, it's usually best to switch topics or end the chat kindly: "Maybe now's not the best time, let's catch up later!" This keeps things positive and leaves space for future conversations.

Most importantly, don't be hard on yourself. Even great communicators run into dead ends or get cold responses; not every conversation will be lively or deep. These moments are just part of talking to real people. Being resilient means not seeing one-word answers as personal failures, but as normal bumps in conversation.

Try to look at these moments with self-compassion. If a conversation falls flat, remind yourself, "Not every conversation will be a home run, and that's okay." This mindset helps reduce anxiety about future talks and keeps you open to new connections. You might want to jot down what was said, how you felt, and what you tried after a tough interaction. Ask yourself, "How could I respond differently next time?" Maybe the person just needed a different setting, or it was simply an off day.

Resilient communication isn't about forcing every chat to go well; it's about bouncing back when things get awkward and remembering that everyone faces these hiccups. With practice, you'll get better at recognizing when someone needs space and when a thoughtful question might help. You'll also learn to take these moments less personally, making social situations less intimidating and letting you enjoy the good conversations that do come your way.

As this chapter wraps up, remember: active listening and empathy are valuable for building connection, even when exchanges are rocky. Every interaction is a chance to practice patience, with yourself and with others. Up next: we'll explore how small shifts in your words and tone can smooth out conversations, making even brief or awkward moments easier and more meaningful.

Chapter Seven

Nonverbal Skills That Speak Louder Than Words

The Confident Posture and Presence at Work and Play

Research shows that standing tall can actually make you feel more confident. The way you hold yourself not only shows your self-assurance but also helps build it.

- Standing with confidence gets you noticed, and anyone can do it.

Power poses became popular because they work. Standing like a superhero, even for a short time, can boost your confidence and lower stress. It might seem odd, but these small changes help. Key takeaways: Doing a power pose before something stressful can make you feel more assertive and perform better. Simple changes, like sitting up straight with your feet flat and hands on the table, show you're capable and can quickly lift your mood. In groups, people notice your presence through your posture before you even say a word.

People form first impressions quickly. If you walk into a room hunched over, with crossed arms or shuffling, others might think you're nervous, even if you're just cold or tired. But if you walk in with your feet hip-width apart, shoulders relaxed, and head up, you'll feel more confident and seem friendlier. Keep your chin level and your arms at your sides. Try not to fidget or cross your arms tightly, since that can make you look closed off or less trustworthy. Be aware that different cultures interpret gestures differently, so adapt your nonverbal cues accordingly.

So what does a confident stance actually look like? In formal situations, stand with your feet under your hips, keep your knees loose, and avoid shifting from side to side. Gently tighten your core and pull your shoulders back. Let your hands rest lightly on the table or at your sides. If you're presenting, stand evenly and try not to sway or pace. In casual settings, like at home or at a concert, you can lean back, but don't slouch, keep your back straight, and feet on the floor. Even when sitting, try not to curl up or cross your arms tightly. These small changes help you look more open and make it easier for others to connect with you.

Meetings often bring out habits like crossing your arms, clicking your pen, checking your phone, or bouncing your knees, which can show you're nervous or impatient. Instead, keep both feet on the floor and let your hands rest loosely, either folded or with palms open, on the table or your lap. Try not to play with objects, since it can distract both you and others.

- Balance confidence and openness in social settings. Relax your shoulders, ground yourself, and breathe to manage nerves.

Use Your Posture Reset Toolkit

Before any important interaction, like an interview, date, group event, or presentation, try the "Wall Test." Stand with your back against a wall so your heels, hips, shoulders, and head all touch it. Notice how tall and open you feel. Step away and try to keep that posture for as long as you can; it's a quick way to reset. If you're short on time, roll your shoulders back three times, stretch your arms overhead while taking a deep breath in, and let them relax as you breathe out. This helps you feel grounded and ready to engage.

Being present is more than just standing tall. It means noticing the mood in the room and matching it, including digital cues like emojis or response times. For example, don't walk into a quiet group or serious meeting acting overly enthusiastic. Instead, relax your muscles and keep your gestures natural, not over-the-top. Pay attention to what others are doing, lean in if they do, or relax if the mood is casual.

Showing you're engaged through your posture is subtle but effective. When joining a conversation, walk up with relaxed shoulders and keep your hands where people can see them. Give a small nod to show you're ready to listen. If you're leading a group, stand with an open posture, uncross your arms, face others, and invite them to join in, either with your body language or by saying something like, "Would love your thoughts!"

Confident posture is about being grounded, present, comfortable with yourself, and respectful to others. Before you walk into any situation, ask yourself: What does this moment need? Am I showing that I'm here and ready to take part? The main point: The more you practice, the more natural and confident your posture will feel, and people will notice your presence even before you say anything.

Mastering Eye Contact Without Feeling Creepy

People often say eye contact is the key to confidence, but it can also feel awkward. It's true that eye contact builds trust and shows you're paying attention, but you need to find the right balance. Too much can feel intense, while too little can seem like you're not interested or are nervous. You don't have to stare; aim for a natural, comfortable rhythm.

What counts as good eye contact depends on the situation. In interviews or formal meetings, you want to look respectful, attentive, and steady, but it's fine to take natural breaks. Give short, genuine looks, then relax your gaze while you listen or think. In casual settings, it's normal to look away more, especially when you're laughing or thinking. People usually copy your eye contact style, which helps set the flow of the conversation. The best conversations often involve meeting someone's eyes as they talk, looking away to think, and then coming back with a smile or nod.

A helpful tip is the "50/70 rule": try to keep eye contact about 50 to 70 percent of the time when talking with someone. Practice maintaining eye contact during conversations to build comfort and confidence. Don't avoid it, but don't overdo it either. When you're speaking, hold eye contact a little longer, then look away when you're thinking or when the topic changes. When you're listening, meet their eyes most of the time, but look away now and then so it doesn't feel too intense. Regular practice helps make natural eye contact feel less awkward and more effective.

- Eye contact should be balanced and natural. Looking away signals reflection, not disrespect. Use a gentle smile or nod to re-engage. Maintain an ebb and flow to keep conversations comfortable rather than confrontational.

Getting used to eye contact takes practice, especially if you're shy or didn't grow up doing it. Start in easy situations, like with friends who won't mind if it feels awkward, and try looking at their eyes for a few seconds at a time. If that's hard, practice in the mirror by talking to yourself and looking into your own eyes. It might feel strange at first, but you'll get used to it. Another tip is to look at the spot between someone's eyebrows instead of directly into their eyes; they usually can't tell, and it makes things less tense for both of you.

If you start to feel anxious during eye contact, focus on your breathing. Inhale slowly while you meet their gaze, and exhale as you look away. This helps you stay relaxed and prevents overthinking. Try practicing in everyday situations, like making eye contact with a cashier when you say thank you, or giving a friendly look to someone on the bus. These small steps will help you get more comfortable over time.

Also, eye contact norms aren't universal. In many Asian and African cultures, direct eye contact can be perceived as rude or confrontational, especially with elders or authority figures. In Western cultures, it's often expected as a sign of honesty. If you're in a multicultural setting or abroad, observe others before defaulting to your own habits. When unsure, mirror the person's level of eye contact.

- Adapt your approach to eye contact. Focus on attention rather than precision; most people won't notice if you look elsewhere. Be honest if maintaining eye contact is difficult, as others typically appreciate your openness and may relax as well.

- Adjust your eye contact if someone seems uncomfortable. Aim for mutual comfort over rigid rules.

Practicing eye contact may feel fake at first, but improvement comes with intention and repetition. If you feel awkward or stumble, smile and proceed. The key takeaway: everyone learns by trying, so don't let discomfort stop you.

Let your eyes bring warmth to your conversations. A soft look, a nod, or a small smile can say a lot. When you find the right balance, not staring, but not looking away too much, you help build trust and make your interactions feel more real.

- Observe eye contact patterns in the media, then apply them in your own interactions to gradually improve your eye contact.

- Eye contact is about genuine connection, not perfection. Adapt to each situation and prioritize presence.

Digital Body Language, Signals in Texts, DMs, and Video Calls

If you've ever wondered how your message came across or noticed someone seemed distracted on a Zoom call, you've experienced digital body language. This is how we show intent, warmth, and presence online, rather than through physical gestures. Today, your digital presence can shape relationships and first impressions just as much as your in-person behavior. Emojis, GIFs, punctuation, how quickly you reply, and how you use your camera all send signals, some subtle, some clear, that really matter.

In texts and DMs, it's hard to tell tone without seeing someone's face or gestures, so digital cues are important. Emojis can replace smiles or nods and show your tone right away. A smiley face is like a grin, and a thumbs-up is a quick way to agree. Punctuation changes the mood: "Sure." feels short, while "Sure!" sounds friendly. GIFs and memes make things playful, but ellipses can add tension or make people wait ("We need to talk..." never feels casual). Short replies like "K" or "Fine" can seem abrupt unless you're close, while longer messages show you care. If you're not sure how your message sounds, read it out loud; what feels neutral to you might come across as harsh on screen.

How quickly you reply also sends a message. Fast replies show you're interested, while slow ones, especially if you don't explain, can make someone feel ignored. If you're busy, a quick note like "Slammed at work, will reply soon!" helps keep things friendly. Try to match the other person's message length and style so the conversation feels natural. Long messages can be too much if the other person isn't doing the same.

On video calls, it takes more effort to show you're engaged because cameras don't capture all your expressions. You don't need to be super animated, but small actions help: nod to show you're listening, use a thumbs-up or wave instead of in-person gestures, and try reaction buttons like clapping or raising your hand to join in without interrupting. Keep your camera at eye level for better eye contact, avoid low angles, and make sure your background isn't distracting. Good lighting and a tidy space help keep the focus on you.

Group chats have their own rules. Tagging someone is like making eye contact; it gets their attention and shows you appreciate them. Welcome new people with a message like "Hey Sarah, welcome!" and use emojis or

GIFs to help them feel included. When you share updates or jokes, give enough background so everyone understands; inside jokes can leave people out or confuse them. If the conversation drifts, bring it back with a prompt like "Circling back to our project...," just like you would in person.

It's easy to misunderstand each other online because tone isn't always clear. Sarcasm can be tricky; without facial expressions, it's often missed or taken the wrong way. If you think a joke might be misunderstood, say so with a note like "Just kidding!" or use a laughing emoji. For sensitive topics like feedback, apologies, or tough news, be clear about your intentions. Saying things like "I want to say this gently," or adding kind words or emojis, can help prevent hurt feelings.

If you think your message didn't come across well, maybe the tone needs to change, or you get a short reply, address it right away. Say something like, "Hope that didn't come across the wrong way!" or "Let me know if I was unclear." This shows you're aware of feelings and helps clear up misunderstandings quickly.

Even small things, like ending with "Thanks!" instead of just your name, using exclamation points to sound friendly (but not too many), or adding line breaks to make your message easier to read, affect how people see your messages. Turning on your camera when others do shows respect, but if you need to keep it off, let people know why. Awkward silences online can feel strange, so fill them with a quick reaction or a short chat message like "Great point!"

In the end, digital body language isn't about being perfect online; it's about being thoughtful and aware of how others might see your messages. Notice both the signals you send and the ones you get. If something seems unclear, clear it up early to avoid problems. Over time, these small habits help make your online interactions warmer, clearer, and more human, even without a handshake or a smile.

Cultural Vibe Checks: Nonverbal Dos and Don'ts Around the World

You might assume a smile, handshake, or nod means the same thing everywhere, but traveling or even moving between neighborhoods shows how much these meanings can change. Many travelers have made mistakes by thinking their body language works everywhere. That's why it's important to do a cultural vibe check, watch, listen, and adjust before connecting. If you've offered a handshake in Japan and got a bow, or tried to hug someone in Sweden and they pulled away, you know how awkward it can feel. These moments happen fast and can leave everyone feeling uncomfortable.

The tricky part is that nonverbal signals vary widely by culture. Greetings set the mood. In the US, a handshake shows respect, especially at work. In Japan, bowing means gratitude, apology, or respect, and how you bow matters. Trying to shake hands there can confuse or make someone uncomfortable. In Latin America, people stand closer, touch more, and even give cheek kisses at work. In Scandinavia, people value personal space, and standing too close can be perceived as rude. Every culture has its own "bubble," and it might be bigger or smaller than what you're used to.

Gestures can be even more confusing. A thumbs-up means approval in the US or Canada, but it's offensive in Greece, Russia, or parts of the Middle East. The "OK" sign is fine in some places, but rude in Brazil. Even waving your hand can be misunderstood; some cultures see it as a call to an animal, not a person. Smiling at strangers is normal in North America, but can seem strange or fake in Russia or Korea. Even though facial expressions like happiness and sadness look the same everywhere, their meanings can vary from place to place.

Eye contact can mean very different things. In many Western countries, it is seen as a sign of confidence and honesty. In much of Asia and Africa, it's more respectful to look down when speaking to elders or those in charge; direct eye contact can seem rude or overly bold. Even though people use their hands differently, Italians use lots of gestures, while the British tend to keep their hands still.

All these differences can feel overwhelming at first. The best thing to do is watch and copy what others do. When you're in a new place, wait and see how locals greet each other, do they touch, bow, nod, or wave? Notice how close they stand to each other. If you're not sure, ask someone you trust, like, "What's the best way to greet here?" People usually appreciate it when you try not to make mistakes.

Also, notice the group's mood before you do anything. In business meetings in other countries, don't be the first to offer a handshake; wait and see how others handle it. At social events, watch if people hug, nod, or do something different when they meet. Being flexible shows respect and helps you build trust quickly.

Mistakes will happen. At an international conference, I once tried to shake hands with an executive who just bowed her head. It felt awkward for a second, but I nodded and smiled, and we both laughed about it later. In Brazil, I stood too far away at a party until people moved closer, showing me that personal space is different there. These slip-ups can feel uncomfortable, but if you handle them with humility, they often become good icebreakers.

Some mistakes can have bigger effects. A colleague of mine lost credibility in Thailand by crossing his legs toward a client; pointing your foot at someone is seen as rude there. He apologized after learning about the custom, and by showing he cared, he was able to fix the relationship.

If you make a mistake (and everyone does), admit it quickly and honestly. Say something like, "Sorry, I'm still learning." Most people appreciate honesty more than stubbornness and will forgive you if they see you want to improve.

The Cultural Vibe Check Framework

- Pause before greeting; observe others first

- Mirror their level of touch or distance

- Ask locals about gestures or greetings if unsure

- Notice facial expressions, are they congruent with words?

- If lost, nod or smile gently, it's rarely offensive

- If you mess up, apologize sincerely and move on

The goal isn't to be perfect, but to be curious and try your best. Every culture has its own way of doing things, and paying attention helps make your interactions easier and more meaningful.

As you move forward, remember that communication is more than just words. Being aware of different cultures helps you build real connections. Next, we'll look at how to handle awkward or tense conversations so you can stay calm in any situation.

Chapter Eight

Navigating Awkward, Difficult, and High-Stakes Conversations

What to Do When You Say Something Embarrassing

Everyone has moments when their words come out wrong, like calling your boss by the wrong name, sharing too much on a date, or telling a joke that falls flat. You might feel your face get hot and wish you could disappear. Pop culture is full of these situations, from Michael Scott's mistakes in "The Office" to awkward viral TikToks. Embarrassment happens to everyone. If you keep thinking about your awkward moments, you're not alone.

Embarrassment can feel intense because of the "spotlight effect." This is when we think our mistakes stand out more than they really do. Most people either move on quickly or are focused on their own mistakes. Knowing this can help, but it doesn't make embarrassment disappear right away. That's why it helps to have a plan for responding.

Start by pausing and taking a deep breath to calm yourself. Admit your mistake, but don't make it a bigger deal than it is. A little humor, like saying "Classic me, putting my foot in my mouth!" can help, but keep it short. If your mistake was bigger, you can say, "That came out wrong, let me try again," or "Sorry, that was awkward, can I rewind for a moment?" This shows you're aware and ready to move on.

If you make a bigger mistake, like sharing too much in a group or saying something off at work, be honest and correct yourself quickly. You can say, "Sorry, that was too much info," or "I misspoke, let me clarify." Pay attention to how others react. If everyone seems fine, keep going. If the mood changes, address it simply and with confidence.

Digital mistakes can be tough, like sending a message to the wrong chat or making a lot of typos. Being honest helps: say "Oops, meant for someone else!" or "Sorry, I misspoke!" If it's a bigger issue, clear things up in private. If no one notices, move on. Apologizing too much only makes it more awkward.

The "Mistake Reset" Exercise

Try this exercise to recover after saying something embarrassing: Pause and take a deep breath. Reset your body by straightening your posture, relaxing your arms, and rolling your shoulders back. This helps you and others see you're ready to move on. Say something short like "Whoops!" or "Well, that's a first!" If needed, give a quick correction, like "Here's what I meant..." Practice this in easy situations so it feels natural when it matters. This helps you bounce back and keep going.

Letting go is often the hardest part. We tend to replay embarrassing moments in our minds, but holding onto them only makes us feel worse. Everyone has awkward stories, so you're not alone. The real success is not in avoiding mistakes, but in bouncing back and moving forward.

The "Clapback" Playbook to Handling Rudeness With Grace

Everyone deals with rude comments in meetings, sarcastic jokes in group chats, or people trying to provoke them online. Rudeness can be direct or hidden behind "just kidding." It's tempting to snap back, but a real clapback means standing your ground, setting boundaries, and staying calm. Being assertive helps you avoid drama and makes your response stand out.

Rude replies are common on social media. The best way to respond is to stay calm, collected, and maybe a little witty, like saying "Thanks for sharing your opinion" or "Interesting perspective!" Direct answers help avoid making things worse. Sometimes, saying nothing at all shows you're not interested in the drama.

Dealing with rudeness starts by noticing what's going on. Is the person just looking for attention? Is there a crowd watching? If they want to provoke you, ignoring them often works best. If someone crosses a line in public, respond calmly without being negative yourself. You can say, "That was a bit harsh. Can we reset?" or "I'd appreciate a more respectful conversation." This way, you address the behavior and encourage better interactions without causing drama.

Redirecting and Setting the Tone

Redirecting the conversation can help. If someone is being sarcastic, you can say, "Let's keep it positive," or "Can we stay on topic?" In busy group chats, set the tone by saying, "Let's keep the convo constructive." Sometimes people don't notice their negativity until you gently point it out. A quick reminder can get things back on track.

Silence can be powerful. You don't have to reply to everyone. If someone is trying to provoke you or just being negative, stepping back often calms things down faster than any comeback.

Responding in Public Spaces

If things get heated on social media or in a meeting, keep your main goal in mind. Are you setting boundaries, supporting someone, or showing that disrespect isn't okay? Adjust your response as needed: say "I don't think that's fair," or "Let's make sure everyone feels respected." Speaking directly and calmly shows strength and maturity.

Dealing With Microaggressions

Microaggressions and passive-aggressive comments are often subtle, like remarks about your accent or backhanded compliments. These moments can make you freeze or doubt yourself. Don't worry about seeming "too sensitive." Responding directly but politely protects your dignity. You can say, "I'm sure you didn't mean it that way, but that felt off," or "Can we clarify what was meant?" This addresses the words, not the person, and encourages them to think twice without starting a conflict.

Online, if you notice microaggressions, whether directed at you or someone else, it's important to speak up. You don't have to start an argument; sometimes saying, "That didn't sit right with me," or "Can we be mindful of how that sounds?" can change the conversation and support others. If speaking up in public feels too hard, send a private message like, "Hey, that comment may have come across as hurtful." This way, you address the issue without extra drama.

Knowing When to Walk Away

Sometimes, the best choice is to walk away, especially if someone won't listen. This isn't a sign of weakness; it's taking care of yourself. Arguing with trolls or people who want conflict drains your energy. Save your effort for conversations where respect is possible.

The Real Power of the Clapback

The real skill in responding to rudeness is to keep your self-respect and communicate assertively. Whether you use a clever reply, set a boundary calmly, redirect the conversation, or choose silence, you decide how much negativity affects your day.

Disagreeing Without Drama and Constructive Conflict in Any Setting

Disagreement isn't always bad or scary. It's actually part of building strong relationships with friends, coworkers, family, or roommates. Real connections grow through healthy challenges. Teams and friendships improve through debate, leading to better outcomes. Progress often begins with a simple, "I see it differently," even if it feels uncomfortable.

The goal isn't to avoid conflict, but to share your view helpfully. Let go of trying to "win" and focus on being curious. Use "I" statements, like "I see it differently because..." or "Here's my perspective..." instead of saying "You're wrong." This makes the conversation feel more personal and less defensive. Ask, "Help me understand your view," to show you want to listen. Saying, "Would you explain your thinking?" can also lower tension and build respect.

Good listening is key during disagreements. Show you're paying attention by repeating back what you heard, like "So you're saying..." or "I understand why you'd feel that way." This shows you understand, even if you don't agree. Avoid saying things like "You always..." or "You never..." since these are rarely true and can make things worse. Instead, use specific examples and facts.

Conflict in Different Settings

When you're debating projects, deadlines, or strategies at work, present your ideas as contributions, not criticisms. You can say, "I appreciate your point, here's another angle..." If things get tense, suggest a break: "Maybe we need time to reflect, can we revisit in ten?"

Roommate disagreements often come up over chores or noise. Instead of blaming, try saying, "I feel stressed when dishes pile up; can we come up with a system?" Sharing your feelings and needs helps you find a solution together.

Family disagreements can be tough because of emotions and past experiences. If things get heated, admit it: "This topic is difficult, can we take a break and revisit?"

Online conversations can get out of hand fast. If group chats or social media discussions become tense, suggest, "Let's agree to disagree and focus on our goals." If things turn toxic, it's better to leave quietly than to keep the negativity going.

Mindset and Tactics

Being curious is important. Ask questions to understand their point of view, like "What influenced your thinking?" or "Is there context I'm missing?" This helps move the conversation away from arguments and toward finding solutions.

Most of the time, people want to feel heard. Listening carefully and showing respect helps everyone relax and makes it easier to solve problems. If emotions start to rise, check in with yourself: take a breath, pay attention to your tone, and relax your body. Say how you feel, like "I'm getting frustrated, I want this to work for both of us." This encourages others to share their feelings too and can help calm things down.

Aiming for Understanding, Not Winning

You won't always agree, and that's okay. What matters most is that both sides feel heard, even if you still disagree. Sometimes, it's enough to set the topic aside and focus on what you have in common. Handling conflict well builds trust and shows you can be honest without hurting others. Over time, these habits make people trust you with difficult conversations, not just the easy ones.

Repairing Conversations That Go Off the Rails

In every heated conversation, there's a moment when you notice things aren't going well. Maybe someone's tone gets sharper, voices get louder, or sarcasm appears. You might see a friend cross their arms or clench their jaw. Sometimes, you both keep repeating the same points and get more frustrated. It can also be as simple as an awkward pause, someone checking their phone, or the energy dropping. Noticing these early signs, like confusion, drifting off topic, or rising emotions, can help you save the conversation before it turns into blame or silence. The sooner you notice things going off track, the easier it is to fix.

When you notice things going off track, it helps to say so directly. You don't have to be stiff or formal. Try saying, "Hey, I feel like we're getting off track, mind if we pause for a second?" or "I think we're missing each other here. Can we take a step back?" These honest phrases reset the conversation and show you care about the other person. It's not about blaming anyone; it's about pointing out that something feels off and inviting a fresh start. Sometimes, saying, "Let's clarify, because I think we're talking past each other," is enough to get everyone back on the same page.

Emotions can build up fast, especially when there are misunderstandings. If you notice your heart racing or your breathing getting quicker, it's harder to listen or speak clearly. That's when it's important to manage your emotions. Permit yourself to slow down. If things get tense, suggest a five-minute break: "Let's grab some water and regroup." Even a short pause can help both people reset. During the break, or even right away, check your posture: drop your shoulders, unclench your fists, and relax your hands. Open body language shows you're ready to find solutions, not to fight.

Breathing exercises can help too. Try box breathing: breathe in for 4 counts, hold for 4, breathe out for 4, and hold again for 4. This simple pattern calms your body and helps you feel more in control before you continue. If you start to feel defensive or overwhelmed, say so: "I need a second to cool down." Showing self-control encourages others to do the same.

Sometimes, even trying to fix things in the moment doesn't work, especially if anger or disappointment lingers after a tough conversation. That's when following up is most important. Reaching out later shows maturity and that you care about fixing things. You could send a quick message: "About earlier, I didn't like how we left things and want to make it right." Or talk in person: "I know our talk got tense. I want to try again tomorrow when we're both less stressed." These actions don't erase what happened, but they show you're committed to the relationship and that tough conversations aren't the end.

You might also need to clear up confusion or hurt feelings by giving more context. You can say, "I realized after our conversation that I wasn't clear about what I meant," or "I want to make sure I understood what you were saying, can we check in?" Sometimes, the best thing is to show up again with kindness and act normal. A little small talk after a tough conversation can help reset the mood and remind everyone that things can get back to normal.

Spotting Trouble Early

Think about a recent conversation that felt tense or confusing. Write down what signs you noticed, like changes in tone, body language, repeated arguments, drifting off topic, or awkward silences. Then, come up with one phrase you could use next time to point out the problem without blaming anyone. Practicing these lines makes it easier to use them when you need to.

Fixing conversations isn't about being perfect. It's about being honest with yourself and others, showing humility when things go wrong, and coming back with empathy and a willingness to try again. That's how trust grows, one small repair at a time.

Assertiveness Skills for Job Interviews, Performance Reviews, and More

Assertiveness isn't about being loud or pushy. It's about finding a balance between holding back and overpowering others. At its heart, assertiveness means clearly sharing your thoughts, needs, and boundaries while still respecting others. This is especially important in situations like job interviews or performance reviews. Being passive might mean agreeing to everything, avoiding eye contact, or not showing your strengths, while being aggressive looks like bragging, interrupting, or focusing only on your own agenda. Assertiveness helps you share your strengths with confidence, without sounding arrogant, and ask questions without seeming defensive.

In job interviews, being assertive could mean saying, "I'm proud of how I led my team through a tough deadline," instead of just saying you helped. Try to show that you're capable and self-aware, not boastful. In performance reviews, be direct: ask, "Could you give me examples of what I did well and areas to improve?" or say, "Looking ahead, I'd like to take on more responsibility and work toward a senior role."

Being prepared is important for assertive communication. The STAR technique, Situation, Task, Action, Result, is a great tool. Before interviews or negotiations, get your STAR stories ready: explain the situation, your role, what you did, and what happened. This helps you provide clear, focused examples. For example, if asked about problem-solving: "Last quarter (Situation), our team had a tight deadline (Task). I reorganized our workflow (Action), helping us deliver two days early (Result)." This method keeps your answers clear and avoids rambling.

Assertive language is clear but still polite. Phrases like "I'd like to discuss..." or "I'm seeking clarity on..." show confidence without sounding demanding. Having a few scripts ready can help in tough moments. For example, if asked, "Why did you leave your last job?" you could say, "I wanted new challenges that match my skills." If feedback is unclear, ask, "Thank you for sharing that. Could you provide a specific example so I can improve?" For salary discussions, say, "Based on my research and contributions, I'd like to discuss compensation." These responses keep things professional and focused on facts rather than emotions.

Your mindset matters as much as your preparation. In stressful situations, you might feel imposter syndrome, the sense that you don't belong. Fight it with short affirmations like, "I'm prepared and have value to offer." Remember, nobody is perfect, and each interview or review is just one conversation, not a final judgment. Visualization helps too: picture yourself speaking confidently and answering questions smoothly before you go in. A few minutes of this mental practice can help you feel more grounded.

If imposter syndrome sticks around, write down your real skills and recent successes, even the small ones. Remember, everyone has doubts sometimes; assertive people show up anyway. You don't need to be perfect; keep making progress.

When you combine facts with clear requests and positive body language, like standing tall, relaxing your hands, and making calm eye contact, you come across as more credible and trustworthy. People respond well to clarity and calmness. They notice confidence when it's paired with respect.

In short, assertiveness helps you in important conversations. It lets you speak up for yourself without going too far or disappearing into the background. You don't have to be outgoing; make small changes in how you speak and think to show up as your best self, even if you're nervous.

As this chapter ends, remember that tough conversations are a normal part of life and can be handled with the right tools. Assertiveness isn't about being loud; it's about making sure you're heard for the right reasons. Next, we'll look at how digital skills can help you connect and make an impact in any setting.

Chapter Nine

Digital Communication Mastery

Texting With Tact to Keep the Conversation Going Without Overthinking

Imagine glancing at your phone, thumb ready to type, and wondering if your last message was too blunt, too long, too full of emojis, or just awkward. You might erase and rewrite your text several times, maybe even search online for the best way to reply to a simple 'hey' or scroll through old chats, analyzing every pause or punctuation. If you've ever found yourself overthinking like this, you're not alone. Texting anxiety is a common feeling, but approaching your messages with a friendly tone can help you feel more at ease and make others more receptive. Digital conversations are full of hidden cues, and without tone or body language, every word can seem more important.

Texting anxiety often comes from wanting to be liked or understood. We worry that typos or emojis might send the wrong message or make us seem boring, so we overthink. For example, a joke with a smiley might be taken seriously, or a short reply might seem dismissive. But most people aren't analyzing your texts closely; they're busy. You don't need to be perfect. Aim for clear and timely messages. Keep it short and friendly. A simple sentence is better than stressing over every word. Use emojis, but keep them to a minimum. Understanding common misunderstandings can help you avoid unnecessary stress and communicate more naturally.

To keep conversations going, try using simple strategies. Bring up something from an earlier chat, like asking, 'Did you watch that show?' This shows you care and helps move things forward. Open-ended questions, such as 'What's the highlight of your week?' keep things interesting. Follow up on things people mention to make the conversation feel more personal.

Try to match the other person's texting pace and message length. Fast replies show you're interested, but slower replies are normal too. Let conversations pause naturally so no one feels rushed to respond right away.

If someone reads your message but doesn't reply, try not to worry or send another message right away. You can say, 'No worries if you're busy!' to keep things casual. If you need to follow up, wait a day and have a real reason to reach out. Avoid making them feel guilty, check in, or share something new.

End conversations on a friendly note rather than stopping abruptly. For example, you could say, 'Gotta run, but this was fun. Let's catch up soon!' This lets the other person know you enjoyed talking and are open to chatting again.

Text Style Self-Check

Look at your last three text conversations and review your replies.

- Did you mirror timing and length?

- Did you use callbacks or open-ended questions?

- Did you end your chats clearly instead of letting them trail off?

Write down one thing you want to try differently this week, maybe overthinking less, using more playful questions, or just replying without second-guessing every word.

Texting is meant to help you connect, not cause stress. Approach conversations like you would in person, be curious, put in some effort, and don't worry about being perfect.

Dealing with Ghost Mode, or How to Handle and Prevent Digital Drop-Offs

Ghosting is when someone suddenly stops replying without explanation. It can happen in dating, friendships, or networking. Try not to let it hurt your confidence; ghosting is common online.

For example, I once shared memes with a new friend for weeks, then they suddenly stopped replying. There was no argument or awkwardness, just silence. I looked back through our chats for a reason, but the truth is, people ghost for many reasons. Sometimes they feel overwhelmed, miss messages, lose interest, don't know what to say, or want to avoid confrontation and think silence is easier. Knowing that ghosting is a common experience can help you feel less rejected and more understanding that it's often not personal. Most digital drop-offs aren't about you; they're about the other person's situation or feelings.

When someone goes silent, think about whether your last message needed a reply or if the conversation was ending or felt tense. Sometimes chats fade out, or people get busy. Most of the time, it's not personal.

To help prevent ghosting, set expectations early by saying, 'I might be slow to reply!' This shows you respect their time and can help both of you feel more comfortable. Leave your messages open, like 'Let me know when you're free!' To make it easier for others to respond. Asking real questions can also foster mutual respect and understanding, making online interactions feel more natural and less stressful.

Getting ghosted can be tough, especially when you're left wondering what happened. If you want to reach out again, send one friendly message like, 'Hey, just thinking of you, hope all's well!' Or 'Would love to catch up when you're free.' Don't make them feel guilty or send lots of follow-ups; one thoughtful note is enough. If they don't reply after that, it's best to accept the silence and focus on other connections. Moving on helps reduce anxiety and keeps your digital interactions positive. Remember, most ghosting isn't personal, and respecting boundaries is key to building confidence in online communication.

If you've ghosted someone, it's best to admit it by saying something like, 'Sorry, I lost track of replies!' Most people appreciate honesty. Being kind and having realistic expectations can make digital conversations easier to handle.

Did the Conversation Really Get Ghosted?

- Was there a real question waiting for an answer?

- Did the convo stall out naturally?

- Has the person gone silent with others?

- Did something big happen in their life?

- Have you sent more than one follow-up?

If most of your answers suggest there's no harm, treat it as normal digital communication. Send one thoughtful follow-up, then focus on people who are actively connecting with you.

Social Media Etiquette, the Dos, Don'ts, and Power Moves

Social media is public, and each platform has its own code of conduct. On Instagram, focus on recent posts and comment genuinely. Reference something relevant when messaging someone. On Twitter, tag relevant people and add new thoughts in replies. On Facebook, check before sharing group photos. On TikTok, credit original creators and add your own twist.

Make your comments and DMs meaningful. Real engagement is better than generic compliments. Be specific, like saying, 'That sunrise is stunning, where was it?' Always give credit to original creators. When you comment, try to add something thoughtful to start a real conversation and support others with your perspective.

The best moves on social media aren't about showing off; they're about supporting others, and that positive energy often comes back to you. Tag someone after an event, like '@Name's talk at #Conference was on point!' to help both of you reach more people. If you see a great post, share it with your own thoughts, quote tweet, or post about it on LinkedIn and explain what you liked. In group chats or work discussions, celebrate others' achievements: 'Congrats to @Name for that project!' Lifting others helps build stronger relationships and boosts your own visibility.

Respecting privacy and boundaries is key to avoiding drama online. Before posting group photos, especially from work or social events, check with everyone before tagging or sharing. Not everyone wants their picture online, and some people prefer to keep friend groups separate. If you're tagged in something you'd rather keep private, ask for it to be removed and do the same for others. Avoid sending DMs late at night unless it's urgent; just because someone is online doesn't mean they want to chat. If someone keeps crossing your boundaries, don't be afraid to mute, unfollow, or block them. That's looking after yourself, not being dramatic.

Unfollowing or blocking someone is just a way to take care of yourself online. You don't have to announce it or explain your reasons; relationships change online just like they do in real life. If someone unfollows you, try not to overthink it or chase after them. Instead, focus on filling your feed with content and people who inspire you. Social media moves quickly, but your online actions last. Try to make every interaction a little better than before.

Social Media Etiquette Cheat Sheet

- **Instagram**: Like and comment on recent posts only; always credit original creators.

- **Twitter/X**: Tag relevant users only; reply with original insights.

- **Facebook**: Ask before posting group photos; check privacy before tagging.

- **TikTok**: Remix with your own twist; always credit creators.

- **Everywhere**: DM with care; respect time zones; don't spam.

- **Boundaries**: Ask before sharing personal info; unfollow/block for self-care.

When you post with purpose, engage thoughtfully, and respect boundaries, you not only maintain a good reputation but also create real chances for connection and mutual respect in every interaction.

Crafting the Perfect Intro Email or LinkedIn DM

Contacting someone you don't know, whether by email or LinkedIn message, can feel intimidating. The goal is to sound professional yet genuine, friendly but not too eager. Many people write long, rambling messages or use generic templates that get ignored. What works best is being yourself, having a clear reason for reaching out, and making it easy for the other person to reply.

Your subject line matters; it's the first thing people notice. Avoid vague lines like 'Introduction' and use something specific, such as 'Quick Intro from [Event/Connection]' or 'Loved Your Article on [Topic].' This makes your purpose clear and increases the chance your message gets read. Start your greeting warmly and directly; 'Hi [Name], hope you're well!' feels more genuine than a formal 'To whom it may concern.' If you have a mutual contact, mention them right away: 'I met [Mutual Connection] at [Event], and they suggested I reach out.' Giving context up front helps you stand out.

Make your opening personal by mentioning something specific from their work, LinkedIn, or a recent post. For example, 'I enjoyed your article on digital marketing trends,' or 'Your talk on remote leadership at the meetup was fantastic.' This shows you've taken the time to learn about them and aren't sending a generic message. Keep your paragraphs short so your message is easy to read, especially on a phone.

Be direct and get to your point quickly. After you introduce yourself, clearly say what you're hoping for, whether it's a quick call, some advice, or feedback. For example, 'Would you be open to a quick call about your experience moving into UX?' or 'I'm considering roles in your industry, could you share a bit about your path?' These kinds of requests are polite, clear, and show you respect their time.

Try to avoid common mistakes. Don't use vague requests like 'I'd love to pick your brain', it's unclear and puts pressure on the other person. Don't include your whole resume or too much personal history, and skip outdated or overly formal language. Always include a clear subject and some context in your email.

Following up takes a bit of care. If you don't get a reply after a week, it's okay to send a gentle reminder, like, 'Just following up in case my earlier note got buried. I totally understand how busy things get.' Keep your follow-ups short and don't pressure them to respond. If you still don't hear back after one more try, politely move on. Sometimes people are just busy or not interested.

Keep track of your outreach, especially if you're networking or job hunting with many people. Use a simple spreadsheet to list names, dates you sent messages, replies, and follow-ups. Color coding, green for active, yellow for waiting, red for no reply, can help you stay organized and avoid messaging someone twice.

Here's a concise template you can use:

- Subject: Quick Intro from [Event/Connection]

- Hi [Name], hope you're well!

- I came across your work on [specific topic/event] and was impressed by [something specific].

- I'm [your role/context], and I'm reaching out because [clear reason/ask].

- Would you be open to a quick chat about [topic] this week or next?

- Thanks for your time, I truly appreciate it.

- Best,

- [Your Name]

A message like this is short, specific, and direct, so it's easy for the other person to read and reply. The more you practice, the better your introductions will get, and you'll build more real connections.

Making Your Voice Heard in Group Chats, Discords, and Slack

Joining a busy group chat or online community can feel a bit like walking into a party where everyone already knows each other. You might worry about saying the wrong thing or being ignored, but you don't need to be the loudest or funniest to be appreciated. Paying attention to the group's vibe and being thoughtful goes a long way. Start by introducing yourself in a way that fits the group. Share something about yourself, like a hobby or unique skill: 'Hey, everyone! I'm Sam, really into gaming and cold brew coffee, excited to connect!' Even a small detail can help you stand out and come across as friendly.

Before starting new topics, spend some time joining in on ongoing conversations. Reply to threads, answer questions, or react to funny stories with an emoji. This shows you care about the group and aren't just there to talk about yourself. As you build rapport, your own posts and questions will feel more natural, and people will be more likely to respond.

Group chat etiquette can differ, but some basics are always helpful. Tag people with '@Name' to get their attention, especially in busy chats. Use threads for side conversations so the main chat stays organized and topics are easy to follow. Always check pinned messages or group rules before posting; they usually explain what's okay and what's not. Ignoring these can make you seem out of touch or inconsiderate.

Keep your messages clear and avoid sending too many in a row. Try to combine your thoughts instead of posting several times. Only share memes, gifs, or unrelated links if that's what the group is about. If you're not sure, ask: 'Hey, is it okay to share off-topic stuff here?'

To stand out in a good way, focus on adding value. Share helpful resources, like, 'Found this article on productivity hacks, might help with our deadline stress.' Ask questions that get people talking, such as, 'How do you all stay motivated working from home?' Celebrate others' successes:

'Congrats on finishing the project, that's awesome!' A bit of positivity helps create a welcoming group atmosphere.

Conflicts and misunderstandings can happen online just like anywhere else. If things get tense or off-topic, try to guide the conversation back: 'Let's keep things friendly and stay on track.' If someone seems confused or left out, help clarify or include them: 'I think [Name] had a question earlier, let's give them a chance.' Welcome new members: 'Welcome [Name], glad you're here! What brings you to this group?' Small gestures like these help make the community feel safe and inclusive.

If disagreements come up, try not to escalate things. Suggest moving intense topics to direct messages if needed. Most people want to feel heard and respected, so focus on that to keep things calm. If you make a mistake, apologize or explain, no one expects you to be perfect.

Whether you're on Slack for work or Discord for a hobby, the best way to stand out is to listen first, then join in with curiosity and kindness. You don't need to take over the conversation or fade into the background; contribute thoughtfully and make room for others, too.

To sum up, digital communication isn't about being the loudest or overthinking every message. It's about making real connections and helping others feel welcome, even in busy spaces. Next, we'll look at how being aware of different cultures and staying adaptable can help you build even stronger connections, both online and offline.

Chapter Ten

Cultural Fluency and Inclusive Connection

Avoiding Accidental Offense

Picture yourself at a friend's dinner party. You go to shake hands, but the other person hesitates, and things feel a bit awkward. Later, you find out that in their culture, physical contact with strangers is rare, so that a handshake might seem too forward. Or maybe you're at a business meeting in another country, and everyone else shows up ten minutes late while you're the only one on time, feeling out of place. These situations can feel uncomfortable, but they're great chances to learn. Being sensitive to culture isn't just for travelers or diplomats; it helps you connect with anyone, anywhere.

You don't have to go far to run into different cultural habits. Even in your own city, what feels normal to you might seem odd or even rude to someone else. For instance, a thumbs-up emoji means "good job" to many Americans, but in some Middle Eastern countries and Greece, it's actually offensive. Humor is different, too; sarcasm is common in the UK but can be misunderstood or seem rude in other places. Being on time is another area where cultures differ. In Germany and Switzerland, punctuality shows respect, but in parts of Latin America and Africa, meetings often start once everyone has arrived.

Some topics need extra care. Talking about politics over dinner might lead to a lively debate in France, but could cause tension in Japan or Singapore. Money is another tricky subject; some Americans are open about salaries, but in other cultures, finances are private. Even asking about someone's marriage or children, which might seem like friendly small talk, can feel uncomfortable where personal matters are kept private.

Gestures and body language can be tricky. In most places, nodding means "yes," but in Bulgaria or Greece, it actually means "no." Waving someone over with your finger might seem fine, but in much of Asia, it's only used for animals. Showing the soles of your shoes or pointing your foot at someone is considered rude in Thailand and the Middle East. Personal space is different, too. Americans often stand at arm's length, while Brazilians and Italians stand closer, so stepping back might seem unfriendly. In Japan, though, standing too close can make people uncomfortable.

So how do you handle these cultural differences? Nobody expects you to know it all, especially if you're new. What really counts is showing curiosity and respect. Before important meetings, look up local business customs or greetings online. If you're joining a multicultural event or working with people from different countries, check the news for any current issues that might be sensitive. This approach can make your audience feel more confident and open to learning.

When you're in a new place, take a moment to watch how locals greet each other-do they hug, bow, shake hands, or nod? Pay attention to their body language, eye contact, and gestures to better interpret cultural cues. Following their lead until you feel at ease can help you navigate interactions more effectively and avoid misunderstandings.

Everyone makes cultural mistakes sometimes. What's important is how you handle them. Don't brush it off or make excuses. Instead, admit your mistake with a simple, honest apology: "I'm so sorry, was that inappropriate here?" This shows you want to do things right and are willing to learn. If someone explains what happened, thank them: "Thanks for letting me know, I want to get it right." Most people value your effort and honesty more than expecting you to be perfect. This can help your audience feel reassured and more comfortable with their own mistakes.

Your Pre-Event "Cultural Sensitivity" Prep

- **Google etiquette**: Check etiquette tips before big events or foreign meetings.

- **Observe first**: Watch locals before jumping in to greet or interact.

- **Check taboo topics**: Research which topics (like politics, religion, or money) to avoid.

- **Mind gestures**: Look up local hand signals and body language.

- **Watch time**: Learn if punctuality is important or relaxed.

- **Respect personal space**: Notice interaction distances and adapt.

- **Apologize openly**: If you slip up, admit it sincerely and thank anyone who helps.

You don't have to memorize every cultural rule. The key takeaway is to show curiosity and humility. Small mistakes are opportunities for learning and connection, not failure.

Small Talk Across Cultures; What Works (and What Doesn't)

Small talk adds flavor to conversations. In some cultures, it's common and expected, while in others, people skip it and get straight to the point. If your comment about the weather doesn't get much response, or someone seems surprised by direct questions, it's probably just a cultural difference. Each place has its own way of making small talk.

In the UK, weather is the reliable opener: "A bit rainy today, isn't it?" works almost anywhere. In Germany, weather talk is dismissed as fluff; Germans prefer direct questions about plans or views. In Brazil, small talk builds warmth; skipping it can come across as rude. Asking about someone's weekend before business is typical and appreciated.

Safe topics help when local norms are unclear. Food is nearly universal; ask about favorite dishes or recommend a café to spark smiles in Tokyo or Toronto. Sports work well; inquire about teams or games. Public events such as festivals, concerts, or fairs are good conversation starters; they're relevant but not too personal.

Some topics may feel intrusive in some regions. In many Middle Eastern and South Asian countries, questions about family or relationships are routine; in Scandinavia or East Asia, they're too personal. Money is almost always touchy; asking about income or property feels rude or boastful. Politics and religion are best skipped; casual debate in one place can feel confrontational elsewhere.

Adapting small talk shows respect. In India, asking about festivals builds rapport. In Japan, mentioning holidays or seasonal changes, like cherry blossoms, signals cultural awareness. In France, food and wine are safe subjects. In South Africa, rugby is a common topic. Tailoring your topics to local customs enhances connection and shows cultural sensitivity.

When uncertain, draw from current events and your environment. Scanning the news before a gathering or meeting gives relevant openers: "I saw there's a parade this weekend; do you usually go?" or "I heard your city opened a new art exhibit; have you seen it?" These show curiosity without prying.

Awkwardness or misunderstandings are common when expectations are misaligned. If a topic lands poorly or conversation stalls, acknowledge gently: "Do people usually discuss this here?" or "Sorry if that's too personal; what do people usually talk about at events like this?" This saves face and puts others at ease.

Sometimes, a change of topic is needed. "I love learning how people connect in different places" conveys openness and lets your conversation partner share comfortably or steer to safer ground.

Humor differs by culture. Sarcasm is popular in Ireland and Australia, but may confuse or offend elsewhere. In Japan or Korea, humor is subtler. If in doubt, observe first or use light, safe comments rather than risky jokes.

Sometimes, silence is comfortable. In Finland, pauses mean people are thinking, not that they're being awkward. In Italy or Spain, energetic conversation is expected; long silences may signal discomfort.

Flexibility and sensitivity help you navigate conversations. If lost in conversation, ask, "What do people usually talk about here?", to show humility and invite assistance. Most appreciate your effort and may enjoy sharing their customs.

Ultimately, small talk invites, not interrogates. Lead with genuine interest, adapt, and keep topics light: food, sports, local festivals, or observations about the setting. Paying attention to local rhythms and adjusting your approach helps you connect anywhere.

The Multicultural Conversation Starter Pack

Meeting people from different backgrounds at a university event, an online meeting, or a neighborhood barbecue can feel stressful. Many people worry about saying the wrong thing, sounding awkward, or being insensitive, especially when cultures differ. The best approach is to mix curiosity with humility. Show interest, but avoid being nosy or talking down to anyone.

Keep conversation starters grounded in what's shared, observed, or happening. Instead of asking about heritage immediately, notice something present. At a potluck, ask: "That looks delicious, what's in it? Did you grow up eating it?" If a celebration comes up, say: "I heard there's excitement for that holiday. What's it like for you?" These openers invite conversation without making anyone feel on display.

Observation-based questions work well because they're rooted in the moment. Notice unique greetings, like bowing or cheek-kissing, and comment: "I noticed the way people greet each other here is different from what I'm used to. Can you tell me more about it?" This approach turns the conversation over to your partner so they can share what they're comfortable with, making you a participant rather than an interrogator.

Focusing on shared experiences is also helpful. Instead of "Where are you from?", which can make people feel stereotyped, ask about your shared context: "How did you end up at this event?" or "What brought you here today?" Such questions let people reveal their own story, including aspects of their cultural background if they wish. Discussing hobbies, foods, or music preferences can also naturally elicit cultural influences.

Practice curious humility by framing questions respectfully, signaling your openness to learning without treating someone's background as a spectacle. For example, "What's something about your culture you wish more people knew?" or "Are there any traditions or holidays that are really special to you?" These open-ended options invite richer responses without demanding them.

Expressing genuine interest when someone shares isn't just polite; it deepens the conversation. Avoid labeling things as "exotic," which can sound patronizing. Instead, try, "That's interesting, I hadn't heard of that before." If you have a similar story from your own experience, share it or ask how they celebrate with friends or family. This keeps things balanced and natural.

If your question makes someone uncomfortable and they respond curtly or seem uneasy, back off gracefully. Acknowledge it: "Sorry, I didn't mean to put you on the spot." Or pivot: "Let's talk about something else. What do you enjoy doing for fun?" The priority is to make sure others feel comfortable and respected, not to extract answers.

Remember that some people might not wish to discuss their backgrounds; maybe they've had to do it too often, or maybe they want to talk about everyday topics. If someone gets animated about a favorite band or movie, pursue that instead.

If things get awkward, don't stress. Everyone stumbles sometimes. You can reset the atmosphere with a lighthearted comment, such as, "I'm always worried about asking the wrong thing," or change the topic. What matters most is your willingness to listen and learn; most people will appreciate the effort more than perfect wording.

Some good multicultural conversation starters include:

- "What's your favorite thing to eat when you're feeling homesick?"

- "Is there a tradition from your childhood you still love?"

- "Are there any local festivals or events I should check out?"

- "What music reminds you of home?"

- "How do people usually spend weekends here?"

- "I love hearing stories. Do you have one about your family or where you grew up?"

These questions are open, giving people control over how much to share, and are specific without being invasive. When uncertain, focus on the event's context, the food, the music, or something happening nearby.

If the chat starts to feel like an interview, relax and share a personal tidbit too. Balancing the exchange shows you want a real connection, not just information.

Pay attention to body language, smiles, posture, and tone. If someone seems enthusiastic, ask follow-ups; if not, keep things lighter.

The real secret is curiosity, respect, showing interest, and giving space. Most people are glad to talk about what matters to them if they feel seen, not judged. Stay relaxed and open, and others often will be, too.

Conversation Starter Brainstorm

Take five minutes to jot down three context-based questions you could ask someone from a different background at your next event or online meetup. Try one at your next opportunity. Note how it went, what helped, what felt awkward, and how you'd adjust next time. This practice will build your confidence and help each multicultural encounter feel more natural and authentic.

Navigating Language Barriers and Translation Apps With Ease

If you've ever sat with someone and realized you only share a few words, you know how tough language barriers can be. It's normal to worry: am I making sense? Will I offend? Will this be awkward? These moments can feel stressful, but they're also where real connections can start. There's nothing wrong with using simple words, speaking slowly, or repeating yourself. The more patient and relaxed you are, the more at ease everyone feels. It's not about being perfect; it's about trying and showing respect. When words don't work, use gestures, facial expressions, and open body language. A smile, a nod, or acting something out can help when words fall short.

With technology at our fingertips, translation apps have become incredible tools for bridging language gaps. Still, it's important to keep your expectations in check. Tools like Google Translate are best for basic exchanges or clarifying single words and short phrases. If you're using a phone at a noisy party or outside on a busy street, text input might be your best bet; voice recognition sometimes struggles with accents or background noise. For casual chats, the voice feature can feel more natural and keep your hands free. But always double-check the translation before showing it; sometimes what comes out is hilariously wrong or just plain confusing. If you're not sure about the accuracy, try looking up each word separately or ask a bilingual friend to help review. Don't rely on apps for sensitive topics or nuanced feelings; machine translations can miss cultural context or subtleties.

When you're talking with someone who doesn't share your first language, or when you're the one struggling to understand, slowing down is key. Use short sentences and avoid slang or idioms that might not translate well. If you sense confusion, try rephrasing what you said more simply or use gestures to support your point. Sometimes it helps to write down keywords or even sketch out what you mean. Visuals can make a huge difference; a quick drawing on a napkin or pointing to a map can clear up confusion faster than repeating yourself.

One trick that works wonders is paraphrasing back what you understood: "So just to make sure I got this right, you're saying the meeting is at 2:00?" This checks for understanding without putting pressure on the other person. You can also encourage your conversation partner to do the same, invite them to repeat key details back, or write down important info if there's any doubt. If you catch a mistake, laugh it off together; it's about communication, not getting every syllable right.

Miscommunications are part of the process, and that's totally normal. If something gets lost in translation and leads to confusion or a funny mix-up, treat it as a shared experience rather than a setback. Most people are grateful for the effort and will join in seeking a solution. Pausing for a moment to clarify shows you care more about understanding than about being "correct." Small misunderstandings often create stories you'll laugh about later.

Patience is your ally here; rushing never helps when breaking through language barriers. If you need to repeat yourself, do it with kindness and without frustration. Keep your tone gentle and encouraging, especially if your conversation partner seems flustered or shy about their language skills. Encourage them by saying things like, "Your [language] is great!" or "I'm still learning too." Mutual encouragement goes a long way.

Sometimes it helps to set yourself little challenges to get comfortable with language barriers. Try having a full conversation using only basic phrases and gestures for five minutes at your next event or while traveling. You'll quickly realize how much can be communicated without advanced vocabulary. Celebrate these small wins; they show you're adaptable and open-minded.

It's also worth keeping in mind that everyone makes mistakes, no matter how experienced they are with languages. The real goal isn't to speak perfectly but to connect sincerely. Some of my favorite stories come from hilarious translation fails or moments when I accidentally invented new words. These aren't mistakes to hide from; they're badges of honor showing that you were willing to try.

Translation apps will keep getting better, but a human connection always matters more than technology's limits. Use every tool available: speak slowly, use simple words, check for understanding, write things down, draw if needed, and don't be afraid of making mistakes. Every effort counts when building bridges across languages.

In the bigger picture, working through language barriers isn't just about survival; it's about expanding your world and building trust with people you might otherwise never know. These moments challenge you to slow down, listen harder, and show up with patience and humor. They remind us that being understood is less about perfect grammar and more about genuine human connection.

As we finish this chapter on cultural fluency and making inclusive connections, remember that every awkward moment and imperfect conversation shows you're trying and learning. Next, we'll bring all these skills together and create a practical guide for turning social challenges into everyday successes, wherever you are and whoever you're with.

Chapter Eleven

Resilience, Growth, and Your Social Playbook

Tracking Your Social Wins with Templates and Digital Tools

We often miss our social successes and focus too much on awkward moments. Our minds tend to highlight mistakes and downplay small wins. By tracking your social wins, you can shift this mindset. Seeing even little progress helps reduce self-doubt and encourages you to keep trying. Noticing your growth can boost your mood and confidence.

How can you keep track of your wins without it feeling like a chore? You can use whatever works best for you, whether that's pen and paper or your phone. If you like writing things down, set aside a notebook or a journal page for your social wins. Each day, jot down a positive interaction, like chatting with a neighbor, sending a follow-up message, or making eye contact with someone new. If you prefer digital tools, apps like Streaks, Habitica, or Notion templates can help you log wins, set reminders, and track your progress. These tools make growth more fun and rewarding by giving you badges and streaks you can see.

Make your tracking system work for you by keeping it simple and motivating. Choose prompts that matter to you. You might count how many new people you talked to, or reflect on questions like, "What felt easier this week?" Use colors or tags for different types of interactions, like orange for work, blue for friends, and green for online chats, to spot patterns. If you like visuals, try a sticker chart on your wall. If you use Notion or Google Sheets, set up columns such as "Date," "Situation," "What Went Well," and "How I Felt Afterward." This helps you notice trends, like tough Mondays or strong finishes to your week.

Tracking is just the first step; make sure to review your progress regularly. Take 5 minutes each week to review your notes or app data. Ask yourself what went well, when you felt most comfortable, and if your strategies worked. The goal isn't to collect gold stars, but to notice patterns and celebrate your effort. Each month, try making a simple chart or infographic using Notion or Canva. This can help you see how many conversations you started, which situations felt best, and where you might want to focus next month. Recognizing your progress can make you feel proud and motivated to keep improving.

End-of-Week Reflection Checklist

- What was my favorite social win this week?

- Which interaction felt easier than before?

- Did I try any new conversation starters or techniques?

- Where did I surprise myself?

- Is there a situation I'd like to approach differently next time?

Take time each week to think about these questions. Regular check-ins help you see your growth and remind you that you are making progress, even if it feels slow.

Tracking your progress isn't just about patting yourself on the back, though you've earned it. It helps quiet self-doubt and gives you proof that you're improving. Your notes can become a highlight reel to look at before big events or when you feel anxious. You'll spot your strengths and find small, practical goals to work on. Maybe you notice you're good at digital chats but want to get better at group conversations, or you feel more confident when you prepare conversation starters. Keep adjusting your tracking system, change prompts, colors, or review routines so it stays helpful. Every win counts, no matter how small. Progress builds over time.

Turning Setbacks Into Comebacks, Reframing Social "Fails"

Growth isn't always steady, especially with social skills. Some weeks, everything goes well, conversations flow, introductions are easy, and jokes land. Other times, you might freeze in a group chat or make a rough first impression. It's a myth that great communicators never make mistakes. Even confident people get tongue-tied, say the wrong thing, or feel out of sync. Social growth is more like a slow climb with ups and downs, not a perfect staircase. Remember, everyone has these moments, even your favorite podcaster or a skilled coworker. It's normal, and it doesn't define your progress.

Resilient people don't try to be perfect. Instead, they focus on how they react after an awkward moment. I use a simple four-step model to turn a social setback into a comeback: pause, reflect, learn, and re-engage. First, pause. Try not to get stuck in self-blame or replay the moment over and over. Notice how you feel and take a breath. Next, reflect. Ask yourself, "What actually happened?" Try to separate the facts from your anxious thoughts. Maybe you didn't really mess up that introduction; perhaps the group was just distracted. What feels big to you might not even register with others.

Find the lesson in what happened. Don't be hard on yourself or pick apart every detail. Ask, "What did I learn?" Maybe you notice you jump in too fast when you're nervous or get flustered if someone interrupts you. Make a note of what you'd try differently next time. Then, re-engage. This is your comeback. Take a small step forward, like sending a follow-up text to someone or planning to try again at the next event. Don't let one setback stop you from moving forward.

If you're still feeling disappointed, try this exercise: Write about a recent awkward moment. List three things you did well, even small ones like making eye contact or just showing up, and one thing you'll change next time. Or, write a letter to your future self from the perspective of someone who has already overcome this challenge. Remind yourself, "Hey, you're stressed now, but look how far we've come. Here's what helped..." Let your future self give you advice and encouragement.

Real-world comeback stories ground these steps in practice. One friend bombed a first conversation with a new work team; he felt excluded and convinced he'd never fit in. After reflecting, he sent an honest message saying he wanted to try again and asked about their favorite local lunch spot to break the ice. The group welcomed him and later invited him out. Another example: someone tried joining a fitness class and was ignored during introductions; she nearly quit. By showing up again and complimenting someone's sneakers before class, she sparked a real conversation and found her place in the group.

Stories like these are common. They show what can happen when you see setbacks as signals to learn, not reasons to stop. If you pause, reflect honestly, learn from the experience, and try again, even in a small way, those tough moments lose their power. They become proof that growth happens, even when things are messy. Social confidence isn't about never making mistakes; it's about getting back up each time with more understanding.

Building Your Personal Conversation Toolkit (Scripts, Scenarios, and Cheatsheets)

Think about the last time you froze in a conversation, not because you didn't have words, but because your mind went blank. That's when having a personal conversation toolkit can help. Imagine a cheat sheet, either on paper or your phone, filled with lines and strategies that fit your style. Instead of scrambling for words or worrying about awkward moments, you'll have ready options for parties, networking, or group chats.

Start by listing your best openers, the ones that have worked for you, like "How do you know the host?" at a party or "What's keeping you busy these days?" at work. Group them by situation, such as social events, work, or online spaces. Add some recovery lines for when you lose your train of thought or make a mistake, like "Sorry, I blanked, can you remind me?" or "That's my bad for interrupting, please finish your thought." For online groups, try quick entries like "This thread moves fast, mind if I jump in?" Keep your toolkit organized so you can find what you need before any interaction.

Make sure your toolkit is easy to use. If you like paper, write your scripts and scenarios on index cards or in a small notebook you can carry with you. If you prefer digital tools, use your phone's notes app to make color-coded lists, green for social, blue for work, orange for online. Create a folder called "Convo Hacks" or "Social Playbook" to keep everything in one place. Some people like using simple digital flowcharts, such as "If conversation stalls, try a compliment or ask about music." Flashcard apps or downloadable PDF cheatsheets are also helpful if you want to review on the go.

Your toolkit works best when you keep it up to date. Lines that felt natural last year might not fit now, so refresh your list often. If an opener works well, like asking about weekend plans, add it to your toolkit. If something feels awkward or doesn't work, replace it. After each conversation, think about what went well and what didn't. Did an opener get a good response, or did a recovery line help? Tracking what works and what doesn't helps your toolkit match your personality, not just generic advice.

Organizing your toolkit visually can make it easier to use, especially when you're nervous. Try making simple charts with scenarios on one side and your best lines on the other. For group chats, a quick chart can help: "If joining late, listen first; if there's a lull, share an observation; if someone looks left out, invite their opinion." Use colors to spot patterns, blue for transitions, yellow for group dynamics, and red for recovery moves. Scenario trees can help you decide what to do: "If the chat goes quiet, mention something in the room or tell a short story; if someone seems distracted, ask about their day." Visual tools can help you stay calm when you're under pressure.

Updating your toolkit helps your conversations feel real and keeps you from sounding scripted. Pay attention to lines that fit your style and feel natural. Watch how others interact, and borrow or adapt lines that work for you. Your toolkit should be flexible and enjoyable, like your favorite playlist, with new options for different situations. Before any event, review your notes so you're prepared instead of scrambling for words.

As you use your toolkit, it will become natural and grow with your experiences. Each good social moment adds a new line, and each awkward one helps you find something to improve. Over time, you'll have a set of scripts, lines, and strategies that sound like you and work in your daily life, not just generic advice, but practical tools for your world.

How to Ask for Feedback, and Use, Real-World Input

Getting feedback from people you trust is one of the fastest ways to grow socially. You might think you know how you come across, but everyone has blind spots. What feels like an awkward silence to you might look like thoughtful listening to someone else, or your high energy might seem overwhelming. Feedback from others helps you see these differences. Asking for feedback can feel scary because you want helpful advice, but worry about criticism. That's normal. Choose people who support you, friends who want you to do well, caring colleagues, or mentors who give helpful feedback without being harsh.

Ask specific questions when you want feedback. Being clear gets better answers than just asking, "How did I do?" At work, you could ask, "What's one thing I did well leading that meeting?" In social settings, try, "Did I seem approachable when we talked at the party?" The more focused your question, the more useful the feedback. With friends, you might ask, "Was there a time I seemed distracted?" or "Did I talk over anyone tonight?" For online chats, send a message like, "Is there anything I could change in my messages to make them clearer?" The goal isn't praise, but honest, practical feedback you can use.

Getting feedback, especially when it surprises you, takes practice. It's easy to get defensive or want to explain yourself, but real growth comes from listening first. Try to keep your body language calm, no sighs or eye rolls, and don't interrupt, even if the feedback feels off. Saying, "Thanks for sharing that, let me think about it," is a good response. Give yourself time to process afterward. Not all feedback needs action; some of it is just opinion. Decide what's helpful and what isn't. If something is unclear or feels unfair, ask for an example or more details instead of dismissing it or letting it bother you.

The best way to use feedback is to focus on one thing at a time until it feels natural. For example, if you learn that you fill every pause in group chats, set a goal to pause before replying this week and see what happens. If your mentor says your stories are too long, practice getting to the point in conversations. Notice which changes feel easier after a few tries. Over time, you'll see patterns, maybe you get the same feedback more than once, or you notice that improving in one area helps your confidence in others.

Keep things practical. After you ask for feedback, write down what you heard and how you felt. Be honest; don't sugarcoat it. What surprised you? What will you try next? If something hurts, write about it and let yourself feel it before moving on, notice which feedback is easier to use and which is still hard to take in. Remember, the goal isn't to be perfect or to please everyone. It's about making small changes that help you be your best in social situations.

Sometimes the best insights come from unexpected people. A quiet coworker might notice how your enthusiasm brings people together, or a friend might point out that you check your phone during conversations. Asking for feedback can feel intimidating, but it's a shortcut to real progress and better connections. The most important thing is to keep asking, keep listening, and not let one tough comment stop you from learning more.

Designing Your Own Confidence-Through-Action Challenge

Real change happens when you take action, not just think about it. Creating your own confidence-through-action challenge is a low-pressure way to push yourself beyond your habits, with no one else setting the rules. The key is to make it fit your life and social goals so it feels motivating and doable. Start by picking a theme that's just outside your comfort zone. Maybe you want to get better at joining groups, feel more comfortable reaching out online, or practice being a bit more open in conversations. Don't overthink it; choose the area that gives you a mix of excitement and nerves.

Once you've picked your focus, make a simple plan for your challenge. For example, if you want to get better at joining groups, set a goal like "join three different group conversations this week." If you want to practice digital outreach, try messaging one new person each afternoon for five days. Decide how long your challenge will last: a week, ten days, or maybe a month if you want more time. Break your goal into small steps. If your goal is to be more open, start by sharing something small about yourself in a low-pressure setting, then build up as you get more comfortable.

Try to spot possible obstacles before they slow you down. Maybe you get nervous and forget your plan, or you lose motivation after a few days.

Set reminders on your phone or put sticky notes where you'll see them. Having someone to check in with, like a friend, or setting calendar alerts can help you stay on track when motivation drops. If you like structure, plan a mid-challenge review: How am I doing? What feels easier? What's still hard? These quick check-ins help you adjust your approach without being too hard on yourself.

Keeping a record of your challenge makes it feel real and helps you notice progress you might miss otherwise. Choose a method that works for you. You could keep a private journal or write quick notes in a phone app. Some people like recording voice memos after each attempt, and hearing yourself talk about what went well or what was hard can be eye-opening. If you're creative, try daily video diaries or short vlogs to capture both the nerves and the wins. If sharing helps you stay motivated, post updates on social media or send "challenge recaps" to a supportive friend.

How you finish your challenge is just as important as the actions you take. Make time to reflect and celebrate. At the end, set aside a moment to look back, maybe with a cup of coffee or music you enjoy. Write down what surprised you, what was hard, and what made you proud. Give yourself credit for every effort; trying matters as much as the result. Reward yourself in a way that feels special, like a favorite meal, a new book, or a relaxing afternoon. If you want, share your biggest lessons with someone supportive, like a friend, mentor, or online group.

This process sets you up for future growth. Each challenge becomes a stepping stone, making the next risk feel less scary. The skills and confidence you gain will help in other parts of your life, too. The goal isn't to change overnight, but to keep moving forward, one small step at a time.

As you finish this chapter, remember that every step you take, big or small, helps you build the resilience and confidence you need to succeed socially. These challenges show that growth is possible, no matter where you begin. With these tools, you're ready to keep building real connections and handle new situations with more ease. Next, you'll learn how to use all these skills for deeper relationships and lasting impact.

Conclusion

You did it. You worked through the pages, exercises, awkward moments, confidence challenges, scripts, and all those "what do I say now?" situations. If you feel even a bit braver than before, that shows your effort, curiosity, and willingness to try something new.

I wrote this book because I know how it feels to be stuck on the edge of a conversation, freeze up in a group, or overthink every word before sending a message. My goal was simple: to help anyone, especially those between 16 and 45, build real social confidence and practical conversation skills, no matter where you start or what your daily life looks like. Whether you want to make new friends, speak up at work, or feel less awkward at parties, I hope this book would be your guide, cheerleader, and toolkit all in one.

Let's pause and look back at what you've done. We started by naming the real challenges of modern conversation, why "just be yourself" isn't always enough, how small talk can feel endless, and how digital life brings its own challenges. We created practical icebreakers for any situation, so you never have to stand in a coffee shop or at a networking event thinking, "I have no idea what to say." We talked honestly about social anxiety and rejection, and worked through small challenges to gently push your comfort zone. We focused on group dynamics, reading a room, joining a chat, and helping others feel included.

But we didn't stop there. We went beyond small talk, learned how to use transition triggers, and invited real stories and deeper conversations. You developed active listening skills and learned to notice signals that words alone can't convey. We covered nonverbal skills, from posture and eye contact to digital cues, so you're ready for any setting, in person or online. You practiced scripts and frameworks for tough conversations, disagreements, and those "help, this is getting awkward" moments. We also explored cross-cultural skills, so you can connect with anyone, anywhere, and avoid mistakes that come from not knowing what you don't know.

Finally, you built your own social playbook. You learned how to track your wins, bounce back from setbacks, get feedback, and create challenges that help you keep growing. Now you have a toolkit you can use before a big meeting, a first date, a group chat, or any situation that makes you a bit nervous.

What's the main takeaway? You now have practical tools like scripts, frameworks, and small challenges for almost any conversation. To deepen your growth, reflect regularly on your progress, identify areas for improvement, and celebrate your successes. This ongoing reflection will help you stay motivated and confident in your journey.

Take a moment to celebrate that. Really. Most people never take the time or find the courage to practice these skills on purpose. If you've tried even a few challenges, written some scripts, or thought about your social wins, you're already ahead of where you began. Recognize this progress to foster pride and motivation.

But let's be honest, this isn't something you do once and forget. Social confidence isn't a badge you earn and keep forever. It's more like a garden that needs care, sunlight, and a bit of weeding from time to time. Every conversation, every risk, and every time you push past what's comfortable are steps forward. Some days will go smoothly, others might feel awkward or even disappointing. That's normal. That's how real progress happens, and setbacks are just part of the learning process.

Here's my challenge for you: pick one thing from this book and try it today. Maybe you start a chat, send a message you've been avoiding, or join a group or micro-challenge that felt scary a month ago. Notice what happens, pay attention to how it feels, and when you succeed, write it down. Sharing your wins can boost confidence and reinforce your ability to grow.

And if you stumble? That's okay. You're human. Use the scripts, recovery plans, and reframing tools you've learned. Ask for feedback. Adjust and try again. Every attempt is a win because it means you're showing up. That's what matters.

Thank you for letting me be part of your journey. I don't take your trust for granted. You've welcomed my stories, my frameworks, and even my sometimes silly metaphors into your life, and I'm grateful. I truly believe you can connect, belong, and thrive, whether you're outgoing, quiet, or somewhere in between.

If you want to keep going, there are more resources, downloadable toolkits, and ways to connect with me and others working on these skills. You'll find details at the end of this book and on my website. You're not alone, and you don't have to figure everything out by yourself.

Here's my final thought: Your conversations, connections, and risks can open doors to new friendships, career success, and real belonging. The main message is to use your voice, curiosity, and kindness now. You don't need to be perfect; start where you are and see what happens.

You've got this. Keep moving forward, and know that I'm cheering you on every step of the way. Your journey matters, and your growth is just beginning.

A Personal Request from the Author

Thank you for reading *It's Easy to Make Conversation.*

If this book helped you feel more prepared, less awkward, or more confident starting and sustaining conversations, I am truly grateful.

Many people quietly struggle with what to say, how to listen, how to enter a group, how to recover from awkward moments, or how to build genuine connections in everyday situations. More people may benefit from the practical tools in this book, but they may never discover them without your help.

If you found this book worthwhile and informative, please consider leaving an honest review. Your review can help another reader recognize the value of this resource and take the first step toward speaking with more confidence, building stronger relationships, and feeling more comfortable in networking, friendship, and work conversations.

Your review does not need to be long. A few sincere sentences about what helped you most can make a meaningful difference.

Thank you for your support, your time, and your willingness to help this message reach the people who need it most.

With appreciation,
George Munson

Acknowledgements

Beohm, R., & Beohm, R. (2026, April 14). *To Recover from Embarrassing Moments, Practice These 3 Things | Rachel Beohm*. Rachel Beohm | Writer, Speaker, Coach. https://www.rachelbeohm.com/to-recover-from-embarrassing-moments-practice-these-three-things/

Berardi, J. (2024, July 13). *Why "Just Be Yourself" can be terrible advice, Here's what to do instead - Change Maker Academy*. Change Maker Academy. https://www.changemakeracademy.com/articles/dont-just-be-yourself/

Brooks, A. W. (2025, January 31). *The elements of meaningful conversation: fewer mirror questions, more Follow-Ups*. Harvard Business School. https://www.library.hbs.edu/working-knowledge/elements-of-meaningful-conversation-fewer-mirror-questions-more-follow-ups

Chandler, A. (2016, July 15). *Face (to face) time: The power of vibes and group dynamics in a digital world*. Getting Smart. https://www.gettingsmart.com/2016/07/15/face-to-face-time-the-power-of-vibes-and-group-dynamics-in-a-digital-world/

Chowdhury, N., & Khandoker, A. H. (2023). The gold-standard treatment for social anxiety disorder: A roadmap for the future. *Frontiers in Psychology, 13*, 1070975. https://doi.org/10.3389/fpsyg.2022.1070975

Hahn, M., & Molinsky, A. (2018, April 12). *How to Recover from a Cultural Faux Pas.* Harvard Business Review. https://hbr.org/2018/04/how-to-recover-from-a-cultural-faux-pas

Handel, S. (2026, April 21). *The Echo Effect: How Repeating People's Words Improves Social Interaction.* The Emotion Machine. https://www.theemotionmachine.com/the-echo-effect-how-repeating-peoples-words-improves-social-interaction/

Hinckley, J. (n.d.). *How clinicians can support neuroplasticity in adults.* S p e e c h P a t h o l o g y . c o m . https://www.speechpathology.com/articles/clinicians-can-support-neuroplasticity-in-20550

Lonczak, H. S., PhD. (2025, July 7). *How to build rapport with clients: 18 examples & questions.* PositivePsychology.com. https://positivepsychology.com/rapport-building/

Lpca, A. O. P. (2025, November 6). *How to practice active listening: 16 Examples & techniques.* PositivePsychology.com. https://positivepsychology.com/active-listening-techniques/

Making conversation with someone who is only giving you short answers | www.succeedsocially.com. (n.d.). https://www.succeedsocially.com/onewordanswers

Malik, I. (2024, December 7). *Gracefully Recovering from Social Faux Pas: Tips for Handling Awkward Moments.* Our Mental Health. https://www.ourmental.health/social-anxiety/gracefully-recovering-from-social-faux-pas-tips-for-handling-awkward-moments

Melody. (2025, March 1). How to be assertive at work Without being a jerk | Melody Wilding. *Melody Wilding.* https://melodywilding.com/how-to-use-assertive-language-at-work/

Nash, J., PhD. (2026, March 28). *How to set healthy boundaries & Build positive relationships.* PositivePsychology.com.

https://positivepsychology.com/great-self-care-setting-healthy-boundarie
s/

Thirdculturenellie, & Thirdculturenellie. (2024, July 4). *How to make friends in a new city*. Third Culture Nellie. https://thirdculturenellie.com/how-to-make-friends-new-city/